High Society

High Society

The Town & Country Picture Album, 1846–1996

EDITED BY

ANTHONY T. MAZZOLA AND FRANK ZACHARY

TEXTS BY KATHLEEN MADDEN

AFTERWORD BY LOUIS AUCHINCLOSS

HARRY N. ABRAMS, INC., PUBLISHERS
IN ASSOCIATION WITH HEARST MAGAZINES

For Hearst Magazines:
ANTHONY T. MAZZOLA & FRANK ZACHARY
Editorial Directors

KATHLEEN MADDEN
Editor

SAMUEL N. ANTUPIT
Design Director

MICHELE MORGAN MAZZOLA
Special Projects Editor

HEATHER CLARK, ELIZABETH CULLY
Assistants to the Editors

ANNE BREZA, VICTORIA GEIBEL, PAGE STARZINGER
Research

MARGRET FRAME, CATHERINE JONES
Research Assistants

LIZ TROVATO
Designer

For Harry N. Abrams, Inc.:
ROBERT MORTON
Project Manager

Library of Congress Cataloging-in-Publication Data

High society: the Town & country picture album, 1846–1996 / edited by
Anthony T. Mazzola and Frank Zachary; texts by Kathleen Madden;
afterword by Louis Auchincloss.
p.   cm.
Includes index.
ISBN 0–8109–3885–5 (clothbound)
1. Upper class—United States—Pictorial works.   2. United States—
Social life and customs—Pictorial works.   I. Mazzola, Anthony T.
II. Zachary, Frank.   III. Madden, Kathleen (Kathleen Ann)   IV. Town
& country (New York, N.Y.)
E161.H54   1996
305.5′2′0973—dc20   96–5528

CONTENTS

FOREWORD

by Anthony T. Mazzola and Frank Zachary

Putting on our best white ties and tails for a coming-out party, cutting the ribbon on a new building at Vanderbilt University, or whooping home a winner at Saratoga: between us, we've spent forty-four years having a wonderful time editing *Town & Country,* and we hope that you'll have an equally entertaining time leafing through these extraordinary photographs from the magazine's pages. *Town & Country,* for the past 150 years, has searched out the eccentric and the intelligent, the gloriously wrought and the simply stylish, to weave a splendid tapestry of the changing skeins of American Society.

Since the magazine's first issue in 1846, the people who've edited *Town & Country* have assigned, cajoled, inspired, threatened, and invented. Supremely talented and sometimes fractious artists, photographers, illustrators, and writers have brought their own special imprints. Imagine photographer Milton Greene atop a ten-foot stepladder in a Chicago ballroom, precariously aiming his camera down on the 1950s debutantes who danced beneath him like flowers in the wind. Ronny Jaques drove his Volkswagen through the snow-covered Italian Alps, his broken right leg in a thigh cast, to chase down the perfect picture of liquid sunshine and seafood risotto in the gardens of the Hotel Cipriani in Venice. To capture the sangfroid of America's top bachelors lounging on the balcony of the "21" Club, autocratic Norman Parkinson once closed down an entire midtown Manhattan block, snarling traffic and fraying tempers. Patrick O'Higgins showered a housebound Colette with roses simply to gain admission. For Slim Aarons's first assignment for the magazine, some forty years ago, he met with then-editor Henry Sell, who told him a pointed story about *Town & Country*'s owner, the legendary William Randolph Hearst. It seems that a dowager came up to Mr. Hearst one day and complained that although he published a great many magazines, there were none, for her taste, that sufficiently focused on nature. At which point Mr. Hearst replied, "My dear lady, alligators love alligators, plants love plants, but people love people. When alligators and plants buy magazines, we'll do a magazine on nature." Slim continued his career at *T & C* with this as his guiding maxim: he photographed only attractive people doing attractive things in attractive places.

The writers and photographers of *Town & Country* have, as a bunch, regularly summoned up their Nikons, their long dresses or navy-blue blazers, and their steeliest resolve to bring out as diverse a magazine as has existed in the past 150 years. But don't miss the able hands beneath the velvet party gloves. The favorite subjects of *Town & Country* are not just the hothouse flowers who've graced the great houses of Newport or Jackson Hole, they've also been the railroad, steel, and Silicon Valley magnates who've made this country what it is, and the generous givers who've made life a little safer, smarter, and more beautiful for each of us. Take some time, as Louis Auchincloss did, to look beneath the surface of these portraits and to really read what's been said about and by the great U.S. families of fortune: there's a good deal beyond city and country landscapes here. With the creative craftsmanship of our editor, Kathleen Madden, and the clear vision of our designer, Sam Antupit, we offer up *Town & Country*'s portrait of the good life over the past 150 years. From international palaces to cattle spreads outside Dallas, from the best-dressed women to the month's best-sellers, after all is said and done, the ingredients of the last 5,000-plus issues have sufficiently intrigued a tough American audience to make *Town & Country* the oldest consumer magazine in existence. One letter to the editor in April 1940 explained it briefly: "Dear Sirs, You run a damned good magazine. It is something to run a magazine like that and keep out the emetic quality that you get in the British weeklies." Signed, "Ernest Hemingway, Havana."

We ourselves might have put it a bit prettier. But we gratefully, joyously acknowledge the success of 150 years.

WHAT A SWELL PARTY

by Kathleen Madden

They all came: Andy Carnegie and Andy Warhol, Mrs. Astor of the Four Hundred, Salvador Dalí, with his pomaded mustaches, and a young Jacqueline Bouvier. Jay Gould's grandkids tooted by in their miniature made-to-order automobiles. Alice Roosevelt, smartly, injected a word or two (as she famously did); so did Evelyn Waugh, Truman Capote, and Mark Twain. For 150 years, *Town & Country* has tossed one swell, swanky party for its readers. Of the thousands of magazines that today scream for attention on American newsstands, only *Scientific American* has had a longer, continuously successful run, and that's by mere months. And still the party goes on. The engraving's changed; so, too, has the monthly cast of attractive characters on the magazine's pages. But the beat and the music and the menu stay inherently unchanged. With this volume, *Town & Country* kicks off its 150th anniversary celebration. What a pretty party it is.

Back in 1846, *Town & Country* founder Nathaniel Parker Willis was a dandy and a dreamer. One of nine children of a poor family from Portland, Maine, Willis sprang from a sternly Puritan household where cards, dancing, and theatergoing were firmly forbidden. After Nathaniel Willis, Sr., moved his brood to Boston in the early 1800s, he became

AN EASY SMILE,
some soft suede gloves, a shiny new car fender to perch on: Miss Florence Weicker takes in the
Piping Rock Horse Show in 1931.

the creator and editor of *Youth's Companion,* the first religious magazine for children, and a deacon at the famed "Brimstone Corner" Park Street Church. Precocious Willis, Jr.'s horizons soon broadened at Boston Latin School, at Andover and Yale. Away from home, he acquired a taste for fancy clothes, fashionable melancholia, mother-of-pearl manners, and rose-scented verses, which he wrote to much college acclaim.

Returned to Boston as a postgraduate, Willis edited collections of flower-bower poetry and started up a doomed *American Monthly Magazine,* in which he shamelessly gossiped about himself and his social doings. "Natty," his nickname, soon reflected Willis's nicety of manner as much as his baptized name. Mrs. Harrison Gray Otis, "the lady autocrat of Boston," took up the bright young gentleman, and his place was made. When business losses did in Willis's first magazine, he bid Boston *adieu* and headed to New York City to find a bigger fame.

In 1831, George Pope Morris, editor of the New York *Mirror,* hired Willis as an assistant. A sentimental popular songwriter himself and a shrewd businessman, Morris served as the perfect grounding force for the flighty, fanciful redheaded young man from Boston. With $500 in scraped-up funds, they staked Willis to a correspondent's post in Europe. And Willis ran with the ball. He had a ball. In his published letters back to the States, he made the Old World sound madly fashionable, artfully romantic, and ever amusing. Willis went to the stately homes, to the toniest affairs, was publicly challenged to a duel (fortuitously called off when his opponent was deemed in the wrong), lived off the generosity of his many wellborn friends, and found himself a wife in the English Miss Mary Stace, daughter of General William Stace of Woolwich.

By the time Willis returned to New York four years later, it was easy to slide into the role of "topmost bright bubble on the wave of the Town." He hosted soirees, balanced the fashionable life on West Fourth Street with rural retreats to a house in Owego Creek, New York. The town and the country both, happily for Willis, became home base. Throughout the early 1840s, Willis and the entrepreneurial Morris became more closely allied in a series of daily papers, with mixed success. But on Saturday, November 21, 1846, now as partners and co-editors, they finally launched *The Home Journal* on a weekly basis. Its sheets were giant-sized, crammed with type telling of the day's important affairs, heralding an

America where an "upper ten thousand" of the affluent and the able would lead the young nation to a level of home-grown culture fully equal to any in Europe. "Our aim," stated the new journal brashly, "will be to instruct, to refine, and to amuse." A half century later, in 1901, the publication was rechristened *Town & Country*.

The face of America in 1846 was hardly genteel. Woodsy Andy Jackson was newly departed; a rugged democracy still held the popular imagination, and the nation was flexing its young expansionist muscles. Texas was newly annexed; Zachary Taylor headed up troops in Mexico; California was soon to become a state. Hudson River painters offered up a richly romantic New World, full of leafy green promise. Longfellow, Washington Irving, and Ralph Waldo Emerson were the names of the day. *The Home Journal* published them all. Edgar Allan Poe was a uniquely American voice long championed by Nathaniel Willis. For a while, he was hired by *The Home Journal* as literary critic. Willis showcased the poet's melancholy verses, promoted his lectures, appealed to readers for funds to aid Poe's young tubercular wife. In 1856, Willis raised subscriptions to rescue the dead poet's remains from a potter's grave in Baltimore.

When aroused, *The Home Journal* could take a vocal stand. It campaigned, through its many years, for uniforms for policemen, tariff protection for American sculptors and painters, temperance and prison reform, and for the founding of the Woman's Hospital and the Metropolitan Opera. When the Civil War broke out, *The Home Journal* vowed to uphold the "Government, the Constitution and the Laws." An American flag soon patriotically appeared near *The Home Journal*'s title, and there were regular antisecession editorials. In Washington, an ill and aging Nathaniel Willis took it upon himself to amuse a restless Mary Todd Lincoln. He dined at family dinners at the White House, rode around Washington with the First Lady in her carriage. When the mounting death tolls made frivolity and fun-loving obscene, *The Home Journal* published barbed warnings to Mrs. Lincoln about the impropriety of her gallivanting.

With peace and Reconstruction came the passing of both George Pope Morris and Nathaniel Willis. Morris's adopted son, Morris Phillips, became *The Home Journal*'s sole owner and editor, ruling the magazine's growing number of pages for more than three decades – from 1867 to 1900. The Gilded Age had dawned in America.

In the 1960s, a hundred years after Nathaniel Willis and Morris Phillips, Igor Cassini took to task all those faint-of-hearts who claimed that Society was dead. "In my opinion," he wrote, "the only way Society could be wiped out would be if all the earth were devastated in a nuclear war. Even then, you can be sure that if there were only three survivors, sooner or later two of them would give a party and not invite the third. The twosome [would] then become the first snobs in the new world, and they would reactivate Society in its most primitive form." On a somewhat more opulent but more local scale, that's exactly what a little lady named Mrs. William B. Astor did in February 1892. She planned a glorious ball in New York; but her reception room in the house at 350 Fifth Avenue (where the Empire State Building now stands) only comfortably held a few hundred. She asked her pal, social arbiter Ward McAllister, to help pare down her list of New York's crème de la crème. At that moment, the Four Hundred was born. Its descendants, a century later, are still riding socially on the distinction. (Even Ward McAllister suddenly understood, at the last moment, the iron-clad power of Mrs. Astor's approval. Realizing he'd somehow left his own name off the list he'd given a New York City newspaper to publish, he rushed around to hastily correct the fatal omission. When the editor claimed there was no more room for additions, McAllister cried, "Leave out any you like as long as it is not mine!")

Society is, at any particular moment, in any one place, whatever anyone decides to make it. In America, inclusion can turn on fine distinctions between "old" and "new" families. Old generally means pre-Civil War, with an extra star or two given to the Colonials. New is, in effect, anyone who's taken recently gained riches and spent them lavishly and publicly. In the Gilded Age after the Civil War, any fortune not based on land-grant soil, like that of the Livingstons, Pells, Morrises, and the Van Rensselaers, one could bet, was nicely new. Ford, Rockefeller, Carnegie, Harriman, Mellon, and Frick all made their fortunes off America's growing industrialization. But, damn, they spent it to great effect. And had a fine time while they did. In the span of two days in 1880, Jay Gould took home a total of twenty-two pictures from New York's Knoedler gallery and hung them in his Manhattan town house from floor to ceiling.

Harry Lehr—heir to Ward McAllister's mantle as arbiter of taste, "walker" of the great ladies, and waspish wit—loved to poke a needle into others' ballooning pretensions. At a time when self-invented or self-appropriated coats of arms were much in vogue, Oliver Belmont chose those of Dunois, the Bastard of Orleans, for the stained-glass windows at his Newport mansion. When Harry Lehr first eyed the beautifully wrought panes, his response was swift. "My dear Oliver," he asked, "why proclaim yourself illegitimate?"

In the first days of the twentieth century, *The Home Journal* took on a new title— *Town & Country*—and, for the first time, reproduced black-and-white photographs. Suddenly, the social names of the Gilded Age acquired equally socially-prominent faces. John D. Rockefeller was no longer simply "America's First Billionaire" and Standard Oil monopoly maker; in *T & C*'s pages, he took on the look of a kindly old fellow, someone who'd attack nothing more than a small golf ball in his cardigan sweater. Mrs. Stuyvesant Fish, that redoubtable dame, turned up on the beach—dressed in black, of course, with bonnet, crocheted gloves, and parasol. Mrs. Theodore Roosevelt posed quietly (tiredly?) in a beige lace dress, while the Roosevelt kids and their irrepressible Dad, Teddy, romped through various highly photogenic outdoor adventures across the American landscape. Society figures would never be quite the same, in their intimidating dignity. But *Town & Country* loved them all, with journalistic abandon.

On the magazine's pages, the boisterous Roosevelt clan truly became America's First Family. When Princess Alice pulled on a smart seal hat and muffler, and straightened her small shoulders, the century's first media star was made. Theodore, Jr., turned up on the Harvard football field in pullover and knickers; Captains Kermit and Archibald Roosevelt made serious-faced young World War I combatants. When Quentin was killed by a German aviator over Château-Thierry, *Town & Country* quietly eulogized the young man and his family's sacrifices to European freedom. In victory or defeat, the Roosevelts always made wonderful copy. Mrs. Roosevelt's White House receptions were covered by *T & C* as familiarly as a favorite aunt's whist parties. "Even the chilly rain could not keep Mrs. Roosevelt's 'indoor garden-party' from being a success," the magazine told readers in 1908. Not only was the great William Jennings Bryan there, with various state governors and wives, but also Mrs. Robert Goelet, of New York, who was visiting her pal Alice Roosevelt Longworth. But "while sundry lawmakers were disporting themselves at the

White House, the wheels of legislation were arrested by lack of sufficient members to make a quorum in the House of Representatives. Speaker Cannon decided that there was nothing to do but to send to the White House for the truant representatives. Hence deputies made their way into the gay throng and laid an authoritative hand on the shoulders of gentlemen in frock coats." Speaker Cannon, *T & C* concluded, "got his quorum."

Before long, *Town & Country* was society's weekly family album, filled with informal news photographs of the rich and the wellborn at play during their off-hours. The Phippses galloped their polo ponies across the magazine's pages; the Biddles gathered at a shooting lodge; the Vanderbilts put social New York on winter sleds at Lake Placid, in the Adirondacks. At Bailey's Beach, Newport, Mrs. Havemeyer and Mrs. Belmont grandly paraded; at Aiken or Bryn Mawr, children proudly displayed their puppies and fat ponies. The men looked dashing, the women's suitings were chic. The art of America at ease was coming into its own on the pages of *Town & Country*.

Grand studio portraits had their appointed places. George Hoyningen-Huene and Baron Adolf de Meyer reflected back, in black and white and infinitely subtle shades of gray, the luxurious fabrics, the glimmering jewels, and the quiet insecurities of, say, J. P. Morgan's daughter, or the exquisitely curved back of Mrs. Philip Lydig. The great Edward Steichen made romantic with Mrs. Earl E. T. Smith's (born Vanderbilt) yards of wedding draperies. But formality was never America's favorite pose. When congratulated on her debutante presentation at the English court, a visiting Consuelo Yznaga laughed ritual off. "Well, you can just imagine me with a tiara on my head and a dirty bit of tulle around my neck," she said, "curtsying to the Queen of England. That's all there is to tell."

But *Town & Country* didn't quite agree. Debutante presentations and coming-out galas were regularly reported in fine detail on its pages. The food, the wine, the guest list, the decorations, the clothes—always, the clothes—were itemized, rhapsodized, and editorialized in each issue. Weddings, likewise, were held up to a public mirror. When a young socially promising couple eloped, the magazine vocally mourned the loss. What about the guests? The gifts? The parents? What a waste of a great chance for a glorious party.

The beauties danced, skated, and promenaded in the pages of *Town & Country*. Some grew up from tender childhood to the life of a young married in *T & C* over the course of the first half of the twentieth century. There was young Jacqueline Bouvier holding her black puppy in her lap in 1939; laughing across the pages as a 1953 Newport bride; dining out in her long white dress with the finely tuxedoed young Senator John Kennedy in New York a few years later. Gloria Vanderbilt first turned up in 1929 as a plump, snow-covered munchkin playing in Central Park. In the 1950s, photographer Richard Avedon enshrined her, with cropped curly hair, as one of his eight "most beautiful women." Doris Duke sparkled on the zebra banquettes at El Morocco in the 1930s, but twenty years earlier had made the saddest-eyed little flower girl that Somerset, New Jersey, had ever witnessed. Irene Castle only had to get her hands on a new spring outfit in the 1920s, and *Town & Country* had a good excuse to run the charming Irene's winsome face once again. The beauties offered up their youth, their smiles, their dreams and dignity to America's scrapbook. They came, stayed for a brief moment, then were quietly replaced by another season's notion of loveliness.

But, boy, these women could dress. A little jersey dress, some soft suede gloves, the perfect strand of pearls: they regularly bought the best and instinctively knew how to wrap it all together effectively. At Santa Anita in the 1930s or at a Connecticut shooting match, their tweeds were enough to make a grown Scotsman weep. These women's cloches were neat and small; their walking shoes ever shiny and well-heeled. By the 1940s, *Town & Country* was regularly asking those very same social women to model credited clothes—Mainbochers, Patous, or Lucien Lelongs, whatever the season offered. Evening dresses were clear favorites, and the women gave these clothes guts and life in a way that later professional models never naturally mastered.

These social women seemed perfectly at ease in their bodies, they were young and vibrant, and they obviously possessed a life beyond any one moment's fashion mode. To them, modeling in *Town & Country* was all a lark. Born to privilege, these all-American birds never sang for their supper.

Following the prevailing mode, married women in *Town & Country,* well into the 1950s, were referred to as "Mrs.," followed by their husband's name. At times, with their spouse's, father's, and forefathers' accomplishments fully detailed, they took on the pose of nicely pedigreed Thoroughbreds. In its earliest days, *Town & Country* quaintly counseled unmarried maidens in the best ways to attract a husband. "Have a good piano, or none," the magazine advised. "Be sure to have a dreadful cold when asked to 'favor the company.' Never leave your curl papers in the drawing room."

But even in those earliest days, *Town & Country* advocated colleges for women and deplored the unequal wages that factory women were regularly paid. Later, the activities of suffragettes were respectfully reported (especially when they went visiting at Mrs. Belmont's in Newport), and the magazine vocally supported the women's vote. The prevailing notion: women of birth were as sensible as men, and would ultimately change absolutely nothing in the political status quo. Girls were as equally up to mathematics and rugged fresh-air sports as America's young male heirs. On *T & C*'s pages, women swung their golf clubs, whacked their tennis balls, and waved their fishing rods with evident relish. By the 1960s, tanned young beauties in European-brief bikinis were proudly preening their well-bred bodies in all the best resorts – Marbella and St.-Tropez, in Acapulco and on the Costa Brava.

Sports were ever part of the good life; and *Town & Country* photographers went to the stakes races, the Westminster dog show, the fishing streams of Montana, and the Ivy League's football fields. They followed the seasonal migrations of millionaires to Aiken and Palm Beach, to Newport, Lenox, and Bar Harbor. The healthy good looks of the English aristocracy were commented on favorably, somewhat enviously, and *T & C* promoted sporting contests of all kinds. Golf was an especial favorite, for good reason: *Town & Country* editor-in-chief Henry Whigham, who guided the magazine during its heyday teens and 1920s, was himself, like his father-in-law before him, an American amateur golf champion. With a few other men of his time, Whigham virtually created, then popularized, the sport of golf in America.

T & C editors were a diverse bunch. There was a German baron, Nicolas de Gunzburg (in the 1940s) and, throughout the 1950s and early sixties, a preacher's son from Wisconsin, the charming Henry Sell, a distant relation of Buffalo Bill Cody. In the 1990s, Pamela Fiori holds the distinction of becoming *Town & Country*'s first female editor-in-chief. She follows on the heels of a literate and ebullient gent from Pittsburgh, Frank

Zachary, who brought to *Town & Country* in the 1970s and 1980s the journalistic bent he'd displayed at a much-beloved *Holiday* magazine, with great effect. Anthony Mazzola, in the mid-sixties, took *T & C* beyond its American home base to embrace the jet set's peripatetic high style. After his successful *T & C* run, Anthony Mazzola went on to become *Harper's Bazaar* editor-in-chief for another twenty-year reign.

The parties that editor-in-chief Harry Bull (and his jazz-harpist wife) regularly tossed at their Manhattan town house in the 1930s and 1940s were mixings of the smart, the artful, and the awfully social. Through the World War II years, Harry Bull brought a love of the arts to *Town & Country* that made the magazine shine with brilliant polish. He ran essays by Simone de Beauvoir, by Colette and Mary McCarthy. Christopher Isherwood's autobiography played itself out in *T & C*'s pages in its entirety, as did Evelyn Waugh's 1940s *Brideshead Revisited,* in four installments. There was, now monthly, a Graham Greene or a William Saroyan story, something from Henry Miller or Tennessee. With the war's refugees came a wealth of newly available talent: the first drawing that Saul Steinberg sold on his arrival in the United States was to *T & C*. Harry Bull commissioned covers from Raoul Dufy, Max Ernst, and Ludwig Bemelmans. In anticipation of the war's inevitable end, Salvador Dalí worked for a full three years on a celebratory *Town & Country* cover. When V-J Day finally arrived, in mid-August 1945, *T & C* proudly published Dalí's own version of Winged Victory.

Town & Country covers passed through a variety of phases through the years; and each era tended to ring with the tone of the times. At the turn of the twentieth century, Great Ladies and American Moguls ruled the day. Andrew Carnegie was cover news; so, too, was Mrs. Astor. Groupings of Roosevelts or Philadelphia Biddles brought to the magazine a reassuringly familial weight. One series of "Great American Mothers," over a period of some months, showed the social ladies of the day sentimentally surrounded by an attractive handful of well-dressed heirs. Who knew what sorts of mothers these women really were? But they were young; they were beautiful; and they were, above all else, fertile. At the start of the 1900s, that was sufficient cause for a cheerful beginning.

In an attempt to raise American consciousness of the finer things in life, *T & C* graced its covers throughout the twenties with tasteful reproductions of parlor paintings, most of them conveniently for sale at various Manhattan art galleries. Following William Randolph Hearst's purchase of the magazine in 1925 color became an increasingly important editorial feature. Under Harry Bull, the possibilities of color reproductions were examined, explored, played out with humor and graphic effect. A pair of free-floating sunglasses reflected back a seductive beach scene; Bemelmans shot off a spray of multicolored Roman candles for a cityside American Fourth of July; the curving arm of a bright red huntsman's jacket heralded the opening of the fall riding season. And always, there was a splash of humor; there was joy.

The gorgeously photogenic faces that are today *T & C* covers were first anticipated in the 1950s. They were the social men and women, the beautiful people, the muscle guys of industry. Mannequins, traditionally, have belonged to other publications. On *T & C* covers, the "models" are real, powerful, and lead powerhouse lives.

And then came the children, the littlest moguls in pint-size. Kids have always had their say, in *T & C*. When the London blitz of World War II brought boatloads of evacuated little ladyships and lordships, the magazine profiled their progress in the New World with serious regard. Asked "What do you like best here?" eight replied the newspaper comics, two voted for ice cream. One unnatural child praised his new local church service. Some British nannies followed their charges to America, and it was not always a joyful migration. When one young Fauntleroy was feted at the Piping Rock Club with fried chicken, the little guy dug in happily. "Cyril," shrieked his highly refined nursemaid. "Cyril, you are *not* to eat with your fingers like these common American children!" That fine lady, the magazine surmised, was soon shipped back to England with her American hosts' best wishes.

Society in America was growing, broadening, quickening its pace of passing fads. "The only qualification is that everyone must be either amusing or divine," laughed *Town & Country,* of modern Society. "The rich, of course, are automatically both amusing and divine." Displaced royalty were ever entertaining; the Duchess of Windsor's traveling tip was to always take along one's own linens, china, and silver flatware. That way, whether in the Bahamas or Palm Beach, she was always prepared. Before World War I, the Czar, Czarina, and littlest Romanovs were photographed with a heart-wrenchingly respectful distance; by the 1950s and 1960s, the European titleds welcomed one to lunch by the pool, or at their new family-run hotel. They were pals.

In the 1950s, the magazine halfheartedly came to praise the new suburbia, "the true embodiment of town and country living." None of it rang true. *Town and Country* never showcased the cunning little Westport cottage; it liked homesteads with some sweep to them—something on the order of Biltmore, the Vanderbilts' North Carolina estate. Summer family digs in Bar Harbor were nice; private islands off the coast of Maine or in the St. Lawrence River were even better. From W. C. Whitney's new New York home, in 1903, to Mick Jagger's Mustique hideaway in the 1990s, *Town & Country* has offered up only those interiors that are splashily, happily, unreal. Isabella Stewart Gardner's Brookline gardens were praised in 1914 for their "simplicity of rustic adornment." That included, of course, the teahouse and Japanese lily pond and the Roman senator's seat of marble. Ari Onassis' yacht, the *Christina,* came with the nice added distinction of Cretan bull tiles from the ruins at Knossos, now gracing the ship's pool. A dance floor that disappeared at the press of a button carried a certain cachet, too.

Sure, *Town & Country* has always been aspirational. The jewels from Harry Winston shine brightly; so, too, do the private Grumman planes. Even the "Fifty Most Available Bachelors" have a nice shopping-spree sense about them: all is done in good fun. As a neat turn, in the 1980s, *T & C* profiled America's "busiest widows." The fact that they were some of America's wealthiest widows was barely mentioned.

Wealth in America has been characterized, and qualified, as simply this: what a bunch of extraordinarily privileged people manage to do with their abundant blessings. In *Town & Country,* through the years, nothing has remained more constant than a celebration of philanthropy. Be it the charity balls, or Mr. Carnegie's gift of American libraries, or the new moguls' funding of cancer research and education, giving is regularly profiled, hailed, and promoted. From the careful rundowns of the giant foundations' resources to praise of "The Most Generous Americans," *Town & Country* ever balances its bounty of goodies with the worthwhile bread.

A family album takes well to a good party, to be sure. But it's the family's heroes and heroines that keep a great American dynasty like *Town & Country* going.

THE GOOD LIFE

In the early 1930s, the moguls of New York City had a new passion—commuting to the office in their own seaplanes. Each day, the likes of Sonny Whitney, Alfred Vanderbilt, Harrison Williams, Henry Morgan, and Marshall Field would take off from their Oyster Bay, Glen Cove, or Northport, Long Island estates and whip into town and their particular places of Wall Street business. Some days, family pilots would do three round trips: take Dad to work, carry in a son or daughter to a private Manhattan school, ferry the good lady to a Broadway matinee or Upper East Side luncheon. But that, of course, was after some of the finer details had been worked out. At first it seems, the seaplanes would land; the magnates would leap to a pier; and, more often than not, they would wind up in the East River. A group of the damp and disheartened finally prevailed on the "air-minded" Mayor LaGuardia to build floating landing ramps at the eastern end of Thirty-first Street and at the foot of Wall Street.

L.A.'s BRIAN MACDONALD *(left)*
turned out for Ascot in 1987. *Above:* On Long Island in 1934, "two young polo players' wives take Dewees Dilworth for another kind of a ride." The "wives": Mrs. Thomas L. Bancroft and Mrs. Robert E. Strawbridge, Jr.

What makes the good life? Most of the people who've appeared in *Town & Country* over the last 150 years would probably say, it's simply what you make it. It's sun and warmth, and a chance to travel, certainly; children and furry dogs and some cultivated flowers and trees. It's eating well and drinking better. Having satisfying work, but also some time for ease. Family, of course. Rugged sports. Finding furniture with a past and clothes with a future. Then possessing the time, good health, and funding to give to charity. The life that's graced the pages of *Town & Country* these years, surely, has been all of these things. With a bit of culture thrown in—and the chance to keep bumping up against some extraordinarily interesting people.

When George W. Vanderbilt completed his palatial Biltmore in the mountain ridges of North Carolina at the turn of the twentieth century, *Town & Country* dubbed it "The First Great American Estate." "In size it compares with the largest estates in England, while in system of management and administration it is far ahead of them. Like most institutions in America, Biltmore has reached a degree of development in less than ten years equal to that reached in similar English establishments in several hundred." The magazine admired the Biltmore turrets, dormers, and high roofs, its flowering azaleas and grazing Jerseys, and also the family's acumen in buying up the surrounding 120,000 acres. Of course, even for a Vanderbilt, life can never be totally perfect. One local owner had stubbornly held on to his four acres. He was not simply cherishing the past: the neighborhood, it seemed, had "improved so much now that the Vanderbilts have moved in."

Sometimes, the good life is simply about those four special acres. Other times, it's the right clubs, resort travel, second and third homes in Newport or Palm Beach. At some moments, it's just about money.

But that, too, is highly relative. In Paris's troubled economy of 1932, all the grandest restaurants, from the Ritz on down, instituted prix fixe lunches. The Ritz's forty franc meal seemed a terrific deal, until one customer informed its manager that he'd heard the Boston Ritz now had a $1 lunch. The hotel man shrieked, "But those are bistro prices!"

I<small>T'S BEEN GRAND.</small>
Opposite: Mrs. Dwight F. Davis pours for her lap pup in 1938 Washington, D.C. A secretary of the navy's daughter, she married the donor of tennis's Davis Cup.

THE GENTS, THE ADDRESS, THE PERFECT APPOINTMENTS.
Above: Frick Byers in 1992 at Hamilton Farm in New Jersey,
home turf of the U.S. Equestrian Team. *Opposite:* In 1983
Palm Beach, Major H. Stanley Cayzer. Perched on the
Rolls's fender is his granddaughter, Caroline.

In 1907 TOWN & COUNTRY. For a home game in New Haven, the Yale reunion class of '97 out-gentlemans the jokers from Harvard by parading as lavender-trousered Beau Brummels through Yale's Vanderbilt Hall.

AND THERE WAS ALWAYS ANOTHER DAY TO SHOP FOR.
Opposite: Mrs. Carroll Kellogg, in 1939, parades by Fifth
Avenue's very correct Jay-Thorpe. *Above:* Mrs. William
Rhinelander Stewart and Mrs. T. Markoe Robertson take
the day at Belmont in 1925.

THEY FOLLOWED THE SUN.
Left: Alfred G. Vanderbilt and
Randolph Hearst relax in
1934 Los Angeles. *Below:* In
1950, the Duke and Duchess
of Windsor were Palm Beach
regulars. *Opposite:* On hand for
opening day at Hialeah in 1930
were Anthony J. Drexel and
Mrs. Gurnee Munn.

S<small>OME RITUALS NEVER CHANGE,</small>
and they stay exquisitely torturous. In 1974, Dyson Hepting and Stephanie Rodgers were dressed for dance class.

THE POLITICS OF SUMMER.
Since 1908, Rockefellers have
vacationed on Maine's Mount
Desert Island. *Opposite:* Nelson's
granddaughters Jennifer and
Ingrid Rockefeller perch
pondside in 1985. *Above:* In
1974, Dallas Pell, daughter of
Rhode Island Senator
Claiborne Pell, in Newport
with her komondor, Isaac.

At the 1911 new london boat races
(*opposite*): Miss Eleanora Sears and
Mr. Harold S. Vanderbilt. *Above:* In 1937,
Princess di San Faustino (born American
Jane Campbell) graces the beach with
protégée Countess Haugwitz-Reventlow
(better known as Barbara Hutton).
As a young girl in very social 1880s
New York, Jane Campbell made sure
there were no blanks on her dance card.
"When that happened," she said,
"I carefully and gracefully fainted away
and was taken home long before
the fatal moment."

THERE WAS NO BEACH LIKE PALM BEACH, HOME TO THE BIGGEST SWELLS. Ready for the first ride by locomotive in 1896 were Philip M. Lydig, Helen Morton, Gladys Vanderbilt, Amy Townsend, Capt. A. T. Rose, Mrs. Cornelius Vanderbilt, Edith Bishop, Thomas Cushing, Edward Livingston, Dudley Winthrop, Craig Wadsworth, Gertrude Vanderbilt, Lispenard Stewart, Harry Payne Whitney, Sybil Sherman, and Cornelius Vanderbilt.

T HE SOCIAL WHIRL.

Opposite: Bachelor governor of Puerto Rico, General Blanton Winship, twirls a guest across the terrace of the governor's palace in 1939. *Above:* Mrs. Payne Whitney, Mrs. Norman de R. Whitehouse, and Mrs. Arthur Scott Burden at the first spring horse meet, in 1908, at Belmont, Long Island. "All motor cars of high degree and of high speed now have their noses turned toward Belmont Park," reported *T & C.* "They go along merrily, or with the grunt of disapproval if the chauffeur turns into roads that lead not to, but away from the races."

At CASTLE PINES, COLORADO, on a perfect day in 1991, the only boats that set sail were small ones. Golf is regularly the sport of choice here.

"As the french say, you can't have an omelette without breaking eggs, and on that drizzling, wretched day, Belmont Park was having an omelette." But in 1930, for the sixty-second running of the Belmont Stakes *(above)*, it was all Mr. William Woodward's Gallant Fox from start to finish. *Opposite:* With briefcase in hand, Henry S. Morgan heads to a day's work at his father's banking house. In 1931, as many as twenty commuters' private planes each day dropped off their passengers at the seaplane ramp at the foot of Wall Street.

O N THE OLD FRONT PORCH.
Above: In Boca Grande, Florida, in 1992, three future moguls plan
a bike trip to the lighthouse—*from left*, Robert Wykoff, Graham
Barrett, and Barclay Lynch. *Opposite:* In 1938, Lady Lindsay, wife
of the British ambassador, takes tea on her Washington veranda.

IN A PRETTIER WORLD.
Above: Conservationists Laurance and Mary Rockefeller in 1992 at Woodstock, Vermont, a
village they've lived in and fought to preserve. *Opposite:* Philanthropist Brooke Astor in
1993 in her Maine cutting garden. The flower garden, said her daughter-in-law Charlene
Marshall, is very much Brooke. "It's so variegated—and, in her interests, so is she."

THE MOGULS

In 1988, Walter Annenberg sold off a chunk of his publishing empire—including *Seventeen* and *TV Guide,* magazines he'd created—to Rupert Murdoch for a cool $3.2 billion. In 1990, Annenberg handed a full $50 million of those profits to the United Negro College Fund. Said Annenberg at the time: "If you want to awaken people to a need, you need an effective statement."

And there lie the two notable sides of American moguls—the givers and takers, models of generosity and good old Yankee acquisitiveness. John D. Rockefeller, the man whose name became synonymous with money, with his son John D., Jr., donated away an estimated billion dollars across the span of the two men's lifetimes. Henry Ford not only

THE MEN WHO MOVED THE NATION.
Proud, handsome, they exuded power, too, on the pages of *Town & Country. Left:* A bearded Andrew Carnegie in 1907 before the grand house that steel built on New York's Fifth Avenue. *Above:* Henry Ford turns a dapper face in 1914. His affordable Model T, in five short years, had transformed the pace of life in America.

gave the nation the assembly line but also the Ford Foundation—today with a philanthropic muscle estimated at more than $2 billion. Moguls, by definition, do nothing on a meager scale. Their private jets, designer jewels, and pleasure palaces are bigger, splashier, more outrageously opulent; their single-mindedness and sense of purpose can be ruthless, but it's always good copy. For 150 years, these are the people who've provided the juice to each *Town & Country* issue. Throughout the 1980s, *T & C* chronicled, each year, the Most Generous Americans; in the 1960s, by contrast, the list was of the fifty most desirable bachelors—who they were, where to find them, how to land them: in effect, a shopping service guide. Later, women moguls like Estée Lauder, Mary Wells Lawrence, and Donna Karan offered achievements that were, like those of the men before them, giant-sized.

Everything in excess: what could be more fun? Witness Isaac Singer, creator of an improved sewing machine, who shocked Americans with his 1862 divorce and publicly fought with his ex over his millions and assorted mistresses. (With wives one and two and various liaisons, Singer fathered twenty-four children in his lifetime.) E. H. Harriman took on financier Stuyvesant Fish, at the turn of the century, initially over a tea-party slight to Mary Harriman by the outspoken Mamie Fish. Harriman went after Fish with the same energy that laid out thousands of miles of railroad tracks across America. "I'll make those people suffer," Harriman claimed, and he proceeded to go after Stuyvesant Fish's Illinois Central Railroad.

Malcolm Forbes in the 1970s and 1980s was popularly tagged the "happiest million-aire"; true or not, he certainly reveled in his collected toys as much as his business acumen. *Town & Country* showcased his priceless pieces of Fabergé, his hot-air balloon ascents, the museums of toy soldiers and Harley-Davidsons.

J. Paul Getty found that being tagged by the press in 1957 as "America's richest man," could change even a Getty's way of life. "From then on," he told *T & C* in 1964, "I was a curiosity only a step or two removed from the world's tallest man or the world's shortest midget. I was a financial freak." But Getty, to the end, always gave a good story.

Aircraft designer, engineer, industry-creator Donald W. Douglas *(opposite)* in 1955, before his DC-7.

Above: **M**r. and Mrs. E.H. Harriman, whose special train crossed the country in a record 71 hours. *Right:* "The world's greatest woman financier," Mrs. Hetty Green. Born Henrietta Howland Robinson in New Bedford, Massachusetts, she maneuvered her inherited wealth through smart deals and parsimony into an estate of more than $100 million. "Financeering is more than a duty with her," *Town & Country* said, with this picture, in 1907. "It is a pleasure, and she allows nothing to interfere with it."

EVERYTHING WAS LARGER
THAN LIFE—THEIR TASTES FOR
ART, FOR ARGUMENT, FOR LIVING.
Clockwise from right: Sewing-machine
maker Isaac Singer, his second wife,
Isabella, and daughter Winnaretta, circa
1870; Mr. and Mrs. J. Pierpont Morgan
take to their carriage in the early days
of the twentieth century. *Left*: John
Jacob Astor of the famous name. (He
was a grandson of the first, fur-trading
John Jacob. His nephew carried on
the tradition as John Jacob IV—
but went down on the *Titanic*.)

HIGH STYLE.
Alfred Gwynne Vanderbilt
takes the reins in 1907. With
him is his wife, Elsie French;
riding behind, his sister
Gladys, later to become
Countess Széchényi.

AMERICAN-BORN MAGNATES TRAVELED BY MANY ROADS.
Above: John D. Rockefeller's partner-treasurer Henry Morrison Flagler rides a turn-of-the-century wicker carriage with his dog, Delos. From St. Augustine to Miami, Flagler laid out the map of modern South Florida—with hotels, roads, utilities, railroads, and newspapers. In 1897, Flagler also gave the state something equally important—at Palm Beach's Breakers Hotel, its first 18-hole golf course. *Right:* Young horsewoman Priscilla St. George, in 1930, hops on the running board by her grandfather, George F. Baker. Financier, philanthropist, chairman of the board of the First National Bank of New York, Baker financed railroads and steel mills and founded (with $6 million) the School of Business Administration at Harvard.

THE COMMUNICATORS. *Right:* Walter H. Annenberg in 1990. The creator of highly successful magazines also heavily invested in higher education and support for the Corporation for Public Broadcasting. *Below, right:* Publisher, land baron, bon vivant Malcolm Forbes in 1976 shows off a favorite Imperial Russian Easter egg made for Czar Nicholas by Carl Fabergé. Among Forbes's other "Capitalist Tools"—the quiet publication each year of the famed *Social Register.*

Aт home, north and south.
Left: John Nicholas Brown, for whose family Brown
University was named. Here, in 1979, he's in the
historic 1786 John Brown House, which he donated
to Providence's Preservation Society. *Above:*
Billionaire entrepreneur and Metromedia, Inc.,
chairman John Kluge proudly presents his
"Albemarle House" in 1987. On a historic Virginia
tract near the old homes of Jefferson and Madison,
Kluge constructed an estate with greenhouses,
stables, a private chapel, and a separate, simple log
cabin, to serve as his at-home office.

THE COLLECTORS.
Top left: Secretary of the Treasury Andrew Mellon in 1929, with his son-in-law, David K.E. Bruce. Mellons have almost single-handedly funded The National Gallery of Art in Washington, D.C. *Above:* In 1916, coal magnate Henry Clay Frick. His robber-baron abode on New York's Fifth Avenue is today The Frick Museum. *Left:* In 1934, William Randolph Hearst takes to the Lido. His San Simeon California estate and private Xanadu was decades in the building.

OIL BILLIONAIRE J. PAUL GETTY
housed his riches at an English stately
home called Sutton Place. Included
among the private treasures there, in
1964, was Peter Paul Rubens's *Diana and
Her Nymphs Departing for the Chase,* on the
wall behind him, plus a Veronese, a
Reynolds, Gainsborough's *Portrait of Lady
Chesterfield,* and *Man with a Knife*
by Rembrandt.

Cosmetics and computers.
In the 1970s and 1980s, America's growth industries showed a
change of face. *Above:* In Palm Beach, in 1974, Estée Lauder,
founder and chairman of the board (since 1946) of Estée Lauder,
Inc. *Right:* Retired I.B.M. chairman Thomas J. Watson, Jr., wife
Olive, and son Thomas J. III take to the slopes at Vail in 1988.

AMERICAN MOGULS, NEW AND OLD.
Above: John D. Rockefeller, with his son John D., Jr., and brother-in-law R. Rudd, of Cleveland, join the 1910 Easter Parade on New York's Fifth Avenue. *Opposite:* John Johnson—the creator of *Ebony* and *Jet*—with his daughter and publishing heir, Linda Johnson Rice, in 1990.

A BLACK TIE AFFAIR

Smoky rooms, moonlight nights, the club of the moment, dances that would seemingly never end: America might be at war or deep in a depression, but there was always, somehow, another invitation in the mail that demanded a thoughtful fashion response. Usually, it was all for a good cause—another night, another party, another necessary trip to the dressmaker. And *Town & Country* would send along a photographer to record it all.

That's not necessarily an easy task. Getting a guy with a camera and overstuffed film bag into a black-tie gala can be considerably tougher than merely snagging an invitation. When the press was barred from big parties, *Town & Country*'s editors turned up, instead,

T HE NIGHTS, THE LIGHTS, THE PROMISE.
Opposite: Dancing elbow-to-elbow in 1959 at the magical Marble House in Newport.
Above: Mr. and Mrs. T. Suffern Tailer (the golfing "Tommy" by fame) go white-tie in 1935.

as old friends. For a century and more, *T & C* has taken readers along to the big charity bashes, the pricey dinner dances, the best tables in any given town, sized up the food, the fashion, the pretty girls, and the bachelor guests. In 1938, Elsa Maxwell found herself seated at table next to a visibly rejuvenated Henry Luce and his wife, Clare Booth. "Her skin is like a camellia's," Elsa reported back. "But her dialogue is not." Elsa, though, was never exactly one to fall for personalities that were sugarcoated. Of Mrs. Luce's dramaturgy she observed: "Her plays show a Joe Louis punch not possessed by most women authors. . . . She'll soon be our Mrs. Molière."

In 1939, *T & C* thoughtfully sketched out a variety of "swizzle tricks" to confound all cocktail-bar companions. (These were also sure tickets to a free drink, should any sucker be found who'd bet against them.) In 1965, there were exact diagrams of the best tables (and who regularly sat at them) at New York's Colony, Côte Basque, El Morocco, and "21." "The best food in Washington, D.C., is at 1600 Pennsylvania Avenue," the magazine reported back in Camelot days. The Kennedy White House got high marks, too, for the bouquets "straight out of the court of Louis XVI," for the Porthault tablecloths and Nobel Prize winners.

Mrs. Astor's "400" Ball, Truman Capote's Black-and-White bash—they pale against the host of silly theme parties that won the hearts of hostesses at turn-of-the-century Newport. There were "baby" parties (with bottles of milky rum punch), sea nymphs carried in on platters, a farmload's worth of humble wheat and homey bales of straw. In the late 1890s, Newporter and trendsetter Harry Lehr invited a hundred dogs to a formal dinner party. Pets received stewed liver and rice, fricassee of bones, and dog biscuits. "It must have been appreciated," writer Ted Burke quoted Mrs. Lehr. "Because the guests ate until they could eat no more. Elisha Dyer's dachshund so overtaxed its capacities that it fell unconscious by its plate and had to be carried home."

They had humor; they partied hard for charity; their dresses and nights were long, long, long. The pictures tell the tale. Who wouldn't want to go along?

Dressed in her best
for a dinner dance to benefit the Boys Club of New York, Marie M. McKim in 1957.

THEY ALL CAME. *Top left:* In 1941, newlyweds Mr. and Mrs. John Jermain Slocum, in the Rainbow Room. *Top:* Heiress Barbara Hutton, 1935, with Raymond Guest and top-hatted Milton W. Holden. *Above:* Mrs. Byron C. Foy *(second from left)* sits one out with Mr. and Mrs. Charles Amory and Mrs. Julien St. C. Chaqueneau at the 1948 New York Botanical Garden Ball. *Left:* Bertrand L. Taylor, William C. Chanler, Mrs. Howard Cushing, and John E. Parsons game for charity, 1935. *Left, above:* At the Russian Naval Ball, the same year, Cordelia Gurnee, Evan Potter, Mrs. George Fitch, Frederick Y. Dalziel, and Mrs. Ruth Waters. *Opposite page:* By candlelight, in 1959, Mr. and Mrs. Edward T. Russell.

"PARIS SMILES AT THE DEPRESSION" SAID THE *T & C* HEADLINE IN 1932.
And just to prove all was well the lovely Mme. Toulgouat *(opposite)* was photographed by Man Ray in Schiaparelli's
dressed-up cotton evening gown. *Above:* Mrs. David Granger's dress, in 1951, was equally "draped in the classic tradition of
ancient Greek statuary" and custom-made at the Elizabeth Arden Salon; diamonds by Harry Winston.

It was carnival in New Orleans,
but the 1958 women could simply be their own beautiful selves. For over 100 years,
the wonderfully dressed have danced at Mardi Gras balls.

Clockwise from top left: Mona (Mrs. Harrison) Williams with Walter Hoving on the Waldorf Astoria's Starlight Roof in 1949; the sublime Louis Armstrong jazzes it with Velma Middleton, in 1957; *from left,* Gene Tunney, Elsa Maxwell (who organized that particular 1933 party), Louis Bromfield, the Marquise de Polignac, and George Gershwin; George Lowther and Lady Wilkins at a New York dance in 1935.

Left: NEW YORK GUESTS OF HONOR
Princess Grace and Prince Rainier in 1959.
Below: at El Morocco in 1935, "Buzz"
Stout and Mrs. Robert Holt. *Below, right:*
Countess Alice Hoyos, in 1935, with
Charles Frisbie-Kenzle. *Below, left:*
Dining in the grand manner in 1957,
Mrs. Paul Kruming, T. Dennie Boardman,
and Senator and Mrs. John F. Kennedy.

THE BELLES PRIMPED, HAD THEIR HAIR DONE,
then posed with great seriousness for *Town & Country*. *Above:* Francise Clow, in 1935, just before leaving
"to spend the winter in a villa outside Havana," as photographed by George Hoyningen-Huene.
Opposite: In honor of the fiftieth anniversary of the Gibson Ball, in 1948, Genevieve Naylor pictured
(from left) Pamela Curran, daughter of Mrs. Frank Gould; Mrs. Alfred Gwynne Vanderbilt, the former Jeanne Murray;
and Mrs. John Sims Kelly, born Brenda Frazier.

THE BALLROOM WAS JAMMED
at New York's Plaza Hotel *(above)* for the 1957 Fête des Roses.
Opposite: In 1991, at the Breakers in Palm Beach, Lavinia Baker Fouquet
(great-granddaughter of the great banker George Baker) and William E. Hutton III
retrace the steps of their ancestors. So there's never any shortage of room
to dance, there are five gilded Breakers ballrooms. Said Mary Lou Whitney:
"The Breakers is the way you want Palm Beach always to be."

Pearls, bare shoulders,
a ready smile—
a certain formula is
clearly at work here.
Above: Anne Kniffin dances
with Spencer B. Meredith, Jr.,
in 1957. *Left:* In 1961,
Mrs. Frederick Cushing,
Mrs. William L. Hutton,
Mrs. Frederick A. Melhado.

Top: In 1956, Mr. and Mrs. Orson D. Munn, Jr., seat between them Mrs. Earl Cyrus Donegan. *Above:* Gianna Todesco shines at Princess Marcella Borghese's 1958 Roman ball. *Left:* Guiding Peter Grimm through the program of the Gala de la Mediterranée in 1959 was Mrs. Lila Tyng.

S KIRTS WERE BIG, DRESS WAISTS WERE SMALL;
and women of a certain sort had multiples of them in their closets.
Above: Mrs. W. Palmer Dixon in 1954. *Opposite:* In 1952, Mrs. Lewis T. Preston.

At new york's "21" club, photographer Norman Parkinson lines up the city's bachelors in 1987: *(from left)* Peter C. Rockefeller, William S. Gillette, Alfred H. (Chappy) Morris, Peter J. M. Moore, Peter M. Pennoyer, Brent Rowan Hyder, Kirk Henckels, Alexander Brokaw Donner, Howard McClintic Love, Jr., Nicolas W. Combemale, F. Warrington Gillet III.

CALUMET FARMS
JOHN T. LUNDY

E. BARRY RYAN

"21"

FIFTIES CITY, FIFTIES COUNTRY—
the style was much the same. *Opposite:* Polly Haywood Ward on a
penthouse terrace overlooking New York's Rockefeller Center in 1952.
Above: In 1958, Mrs. E. T. Bedford Davie at home in Palm Beach.

Bridge, anyone?

Above: With Boston poet John Wheelwright in 1933 were Mrs. Edward J. Mathews, Mrs. Charles P. Grimes, and Miss Gladys Livermore. *Left:* Updated evenings, in 1990, Chicago's Tony and Robin Armour; her dress by Halston.

THE PARTY'S OVER.
Above: In 1949, Mr. and Mrs. John Wright, Mr. and Mrs. Ira Washburn, and
Mrs. Wainwright on the steps at East Hampton's Maidstone Club.
Opposite: Dawn's early light.

HOLLYWOOD STYLE

The wonderfully worldly Ludwig Bemelmans—humorist, author, observer, illustrator of enormous charm—contributed regularly to *Town & Country* from the 1930s to the 1950s. During 1945, when he spent a year as a writer under contract to MGM, Bemelmans sent in to the magazine long, chatty discursions on the Hollywood character. "Black and white have a thousand shadings here," wrote Bemelmans, "and, while all things have strong scents, you need the nose of a pig to uproot the truffles." And Bemelmans, if anyone, knew a truffle from a toadstool.

Disgusted by the inattention he first received at the studio, he readied his resignation and, in a small bit of spite, painted a somewhat obscene depiction of two MGM lions on

Bᴇᴛᴛᴇ Dᴀᴠɪꜱ ᴍᴏᴅᴇʟᴇᴅ ɪɴ 1949
"a town and travel coat of exceptional design." *Above:* In 1918, the triumvirate of Doug Fairbanks,
Mary Pickford, and Charlie Chaplin toured America to promote the sale of World War I Liberty Bonds.

his office wall. When an unexpected invitation to lunch in the upstairs executive dining room arrived—and when Bemelmans found himself seated next to an appreciative Louis B. Mayer—suddenly his wall work of art was a bit, well, incriminating. Unable to erase it, Bemelmans changed the lions to tigers. Upon seeing the offending artwork, Mr. Mayer's only response was, "Put a frame around it. It's a nice picture." But why, the great moving-picture czar asked, "don't you make lions out of them?"

Bemelmans knew a simple truth about America's social characters in the 1930s, and it's true today as well: the uppercrust dearly loves Hollywood. Oh, *The Social Register* may have dropped Jane Wyatt (born a Van Rensselaer) from its pages when she started acting, or TV star Harry Hamlin for the same reason a half century later. Those are the prickly details. When the great Marjorie Merriweather Post's daughter, Dina Merrill, headed to Tinseltown, *Town & Country* happily followed her. Today, Glenn Close, Mrs. Post's step-granddaughter, does quite nicely, thank you, without bringing bloodlines into the picture.

But in Hollywood's earliest heydays, all was golden. And it made for glorious pictures. Stars met and mingled, they played at being rich, they redefined American glamour and brought a refreshing breeze into society's drawing rooms. *T & C* loved them all: Leslie Howard, with his polo ponies; Clark Gable, Hollywood he-man who could fill out a tux with the best of them; Katharine Hepburn (correctly born a Houghton), improving her golf stroke at the Bel-Air Country Club. *T & C* followed the social stars to Santa Anita, in the 1930s days when both men *and* women wore suits and hats to the track; it carefully detailed the seating plan at Romanoff's. Ina Claire called in to explain how very beautiful Kansas City looked from the air on her first aeroplane flight East; Ingrid Bergman provided the perfect backdrop to Dior's runway collection in 1957 Paris.

What's Hollywood? To quote photographer Slim Aarons, "attractive people doing attractive things in attractive places." "Oh, it's whatever it is, more so than it is anywhere in the world," said Bemelmans. "All is so and so is nothing in Hollywood."

EVERY STAR HAS A STORY.
When aspiring actress Greta Garbo walked into Arnold Genthe's studio in 1925,
the photographer exclaimed, "I don't believe you're real!" She was; but the studios were paying no attention.
Genthe sent a messenger with this picture; Garbo's career began.

BEAUTY, OLD AND NEW.
Above: Model/actress
Isabella Rossellini in 1993.
Right: Isabella's mother,
Ingrid Bergman, takes in the
offerings on Dior's 1957
runway. Bergman had stopped
off in Paris to shop after
picking up a New York Film
Critics' Award for *Anastasia*.

H OLLYWOOD'S STARS
have long done star turns as models, and the clothes
they presented on the pages of *Town & Country* were
invariably picked to match the persona the actress
regularly presented to her eager fans.
Above: Judy Garland made the quintessential
American sweater girl in 1945. *Opposite:* Two years
later, Merle Oberon went grandly classical for
photographer Jean Moral in Madame Grès.

THEY KNEW ABOUT GLAMOUR.
Right: In 1933 Barbara
Stanwyck lounged in satin.
Above: Joan Crawford showed
off her newly remodeled Fifth
Avenue apartment in 1958.
Its eighteen rooms had been
coverted into just nine "alive,
spacious, and sunny" spaces.
One entire glass-shelved
closet was reserved for hats.

In 1956, ALFRED HITCHCOCK
takes a last look at the ground in New York from his
airplane seat. *T & C*'s lovingly concise characterization
of his face and figure: "a pear balanced on a pear."
Opposite: Orson Welles, photographed by George Platt
Lynes in 1937. By the age of 22, Welles had already
earned credits as a "child actor with the Chicago
Opera, animal impersonator in a department store,
music student, Irish landscape painter, actor
with the Gate and Abbey theatres in Dublin, traveler
in Africa, playwright, collaborator in a textbook
on Shakespeare, and radio actor."

THEY DINED, THEY DANCED, they turned up in *Town & Country*. *Left:* Mr. and Mrs. Randolph Scott toured a starlit, outdoor dance floor in 1949. *Above:* Ten years later, society girl-cum-actress Dina Merrill dines at New York's Le Pavillion with Cary Grant.

REX HARRISON
and wife Lilli Palmer (*above*) visit the United Nations in 1951. Why there?
Mr. Harrison wanted photographer Ronny Jaques to shoot him outdoors so his thinning hair
could be dapperly hatted. *Opposite:* Olivia de Havilland arrived for lunch with Maurice Chevalier
one day in 1958 at Chevalier's villa, La Louque in France. Before lunch, at Chevalier's
insistence, she modeled three dresses she'd had fitted that morning at Christian Dior.

HOLLYWOOD may have spelled tinsel to some, but it photographed in pure gold for *Town & Country*. *Right:* Katharine Hepburn picnics in Connecticut in 1969 with photographer Jerome Zerbe. *Above:* Louise Brooks takes her pup to the beach in 1933.

Clockwise from left: Ina Claire
and husband John Gilbert
on their way to Europe in
1929; in 1935, Leslie Howard
presented his polo ponies;
Mr. and Mrs. Bing Crosby
track their land in Baja,
California, in 1962;
Miss Lillian Gish, in the
early 1920s, visits friend
Mrs. Charles H. Duell
in Newport.

Sometimes, the rationale
for an appealing fashion photo
was remarkably thin. *Above:* Marlene Dietrich, in 1944,
solemnly surveys French artist Bernard Lamotte's new
collection of scarves for Lord & Taylor. *Right:* A sultry
Tallulah Bankhead rests between rehearsals for
The Skin of Our Teeth on Wamsutta Supercale sheets
"in white, with blue bowknots."

TIME OFF.
Fred and sister Adele Astaire drop down to the Atlantic Beach Club on a Sunday in 1931 when they had
no Broadway duties in *The Band Wagon*.

Clockwise from left: The sun shines on Pola Negri in 1928 Deauville; Al Jolson and wife Ruby Keeler take lunch at the Santa Anita track in 1935; Governor and Mrs. Ronald Reagan survey the scene in 1972 Acapulco; Warner Baxter, Ronald Colman, and Elizabeth Allan watch a 1934 tennis match.

Director John Huston
arrived in Puerto Vallarta, Mexico *(opposite)* in 1963 to
direct *Night of the Iguana;* by 1980 he had "stayed on and on." *Above:* The next generation
of Hustons, daughter/actress Angelica, photographed by Matthew Rolston for
T & C in 1994. "There's a certain advantage to being well bred, as in racehorses and fine
bloodlines," said Huston. "Wellbred but not overbred." And "If you've had all the
advantages, bad manners are unforgivable."

FORMAL INTRODUCTIONS

If a budding beauty from the right family was available in the first half of the century, there was a clear need for an eligible bridegroom. And there was never a better pathway to a liaison than a coming-out season: twelve months of debutante dances, flattering dresses, and sufficient time to polish rough adolescent edges before entering a more serious social world. Alice Roosevelt had her "season," so did Charlotte Ford and Jacqueline Bouvier. Tricia Nixon did, too. Some seasons were more successful than others.

DEBUT FORMULA—A BEAUTIFUL GIRL AND A ONE-OF-A-KIND DRESS.
Left: The music was supplied by Lester Lanin (seen chatting with Gillian Fuller in 1964). *Above:* Then there are the very necessary young men. In 1950, Sarah Lawrence freshman Joan Neuberger got masculine support from Crowell Baker and John Kean.

In 1964 alone, *Town & Country* reported, some 5,000 eighteen-year-old girls made formal bows to American society in various U.S. cities. Band leader Lester Lanin was booked by anxious parents a dozen years in advance for daughters' coming-out parties. For *T & C* George Christy wrote about the state of "Sex and the Deb" in the physically precocious 1960s. By 1973, the view had changed. "In the days of Women's Lib," said Washington's Sally Quinn, "the whole idea of being put on that kind of display is demeaning." The 1970s were a dicey time for tradition. When emotions run high over all parental beliefs, it's tough to make a convincing case for black ties and long party dresses.

That wasn't the way it was in 1938. "Bow's a Wow," said the *New York Daily News* when the wildly photogenic heiress Brenda Diana Duff Frazier made her debut to society, and danced across the pages of *Town & Country* with high style. Debuts, in any given season, are as much the stories of individual women as of the accepted assemblies: the Saint Cecilia Ball (begun in 1762, in Charleston); the Infirmary Ball in New York City and the New York Junior Assembly; the Veiled Prophet Ball, which has been a St. Louis tradition since 1878.

Other great moments in American debdom: Doris Duke, the richest girl in the world, bows in 1930 in Newport and at Buckingham Palace. Elizabeth II puts an end to presentations at court in 1958, thereby effectively squelching Americans' noble aspirations. Fifty thousand roses and Ella Fitzgerald's singing to 1,200 guests run up the bill to a widely reported $250,000 on Anne Ford's coming-out in 1961.

Asked what makes a terrific party, Lester Lanin responded in 1964, "fabulous music, a spacious dance floor, free access to several bars, and five men to two women." And be kind, Lanin advised aspiring debutantes, to all aging fathers. "Men love being fussed over and fathers, especially, never tire of polishing the parquet with their adorable daughters." The formula remains.

ALEXANDRA VILLARD
in 1964 modeling silk organza trimmed with lace.

THE BUDS IN FIRST FULL BLOOM.
Five members of the Debutante Cotillion rehearse for the
Christmas Ball at the Waldorf in 1951. *Clockwise from bottom*
are Ann Firestone, Venetia Arlen, Mary Audrey Weicker,
Sarane Hickox, and Peggy Hitchcock.

Rites of this particular passage have altered very little through the years.
Opposite: In 1992, deb Cornelia Mai Ercklentz surrounded
herself with properly white-tied and tailed ushers and escorts for the
Infirmary Ball, a New York City social institution, which benefits each year
the New York Downtown Hospital. *Above:* The same year, the same
formula—but in California. The thirtieth annual gala's proceeds went to the
Pasadena Guild of Childrens Hospital in Los Angeles.

H OW LOVELY THEY WERE.
The year was 1933, the nation was hardly at its most hopeful, but the young
women still came of age in the ways of their parents. *Above:* Rose O'Neill Winslow
made her debut in Newport. *Opposite:* Sisters Joan and Katherine Blake were
presented to society at a supper dance at the Ritz Hotel.

THE LESS-THAN-
MERRY MAIDENS
of the early century.
Opposite: Marie Rodewald in
1913. *Clockwise from right:*
Margaret Wagstaff; Mildred
Mordaunt, also both in 1913;
in 1928, debutante Janet
Newbold looks back
to an even earlier era.

THE STAG LINE FORMS
in the Grand Ballroom of
New York's Plaza Hotel (*above*)
for the 1962 Gotham Ball.
Right: The prize—and prime
deb—of that season, the
beautiful Babe Paley's young
daughter, Amanda Jay
Mortimer. Her dress is by
Mainbocher.

E ACH CITY HAS ITS
OWN ASSEMBLY.
Above: A boxful of debs and
escorts at the 1950 Spring
Dinner Dance held at Boston's
Copley Plaza Hotel. *Left:* In
Charlotte, North Carolina,
that same year, the aim was to
recreate the aura of the antebellum South, with sufficient
sweeping skirts and bare
shoulders to warm the heart
of any Southern gentleman.

The dads dressed up, paid up, provided an arm, and proudly presented their daughters to the world. *Left:* Pamela Redfearn and her father in 1962 Rye, New York. *Below:* Ralph Van Inwegen Burdick, Jr., presents his twin daughters in 1971 at Saratoga Springs.

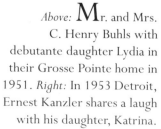

Above: Mr. and Mrs. C. Henry Buhls with debutante daughter Lydia in their Grosse Pointe home in 1951. *Right:* In 1953 Detroit, Ernest Kanzler shares a laugh with his daughter, Katrina.

A CHICAGO DOUBLEHEADER, 1961.
Left: Martha McCormick, daughter of Mr. and Mrs. Brooks McCormick.
Right: Abra Rockefeller Prentice, daughter of Mr. and Mrs. J. Rockefeller Prentice.

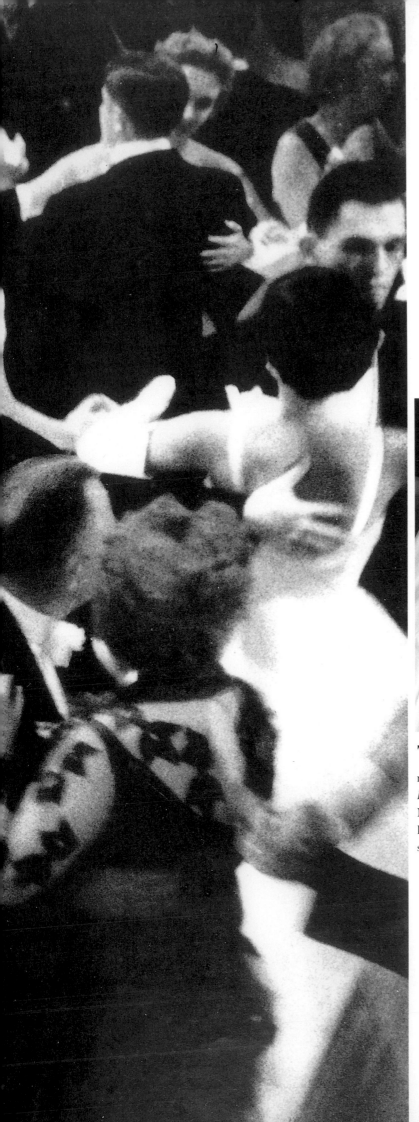

THE NIGHTS WERE SHINING;
nights went on 'til dawn.
Left: The dance floor in
New York in 1955. *Above:*
In 1956, Daphne Bagley
stoops to conquer.

GRANDE DAMES

T heir strands of pearls were longer (and visibly finer) than everyone else's; their upper lips were decidedly stiffer. These old girls set the rules, among their set, of what was acceptable social behavior. "Acceptable," that is, for everyone else: by virtue of their lineage and longevity, these women, through America's eras, could act any way that damn well pleased them.

Traditionally, the old adage goes, women take power where they can find it. In nineteenth-century New York (and well into the twentieth), for women of breeding that meant,

AMERICAN MOGULS OF ANOTHER SORT.

Above: Alice Roosevelt Longworth ruled D.C. with her pithy observations and WASP-ish tongue. *Left:* Joan Whitney Payson gustily supported her baseball team, the New York Mets: "I don't call them a possession," said Mrs. Payson in 1970. "They belong to the City of New York." So, too, did Mrs. Payson.

first and foremost, directing an extended family. Husbands, children, servants, relations near and far all fell within a powerful woman's realm. Then came the possibilities offered in a larger world: reigning over the balls and tea tables; nurturing promising young women into springboard spots for advantageous marriages; keeping a circle of acquaintances and social contacts in line with standards of polite intercourse. Some women—richer, tougher, smarter, perhaps a bit more impervious—rose notably to the occasion.

Pampered, sometimes extravagant spenders, most still possessed a very clear head for household accountings. And many a grande dame has quietly (or not so) held sway over a family financial empire. New England–born heiress and financier Hetty Green rode public buses, wore the same serviceable black dress always, fussed over her various lap dogs—and, at her death in 1916, left an estate considerably larger than J. P. Morgan's. Abby Aldrich Rockefeller, along with Lillie P. Bliss and Mrs. Cornelius J. Sullivan, marshaled sufficient forces to make the Museum of Modern Art in New York a reality in 1929.

And, always, the old girls had style. No one could present a cascading chestful of emeralds quite like Mrs. Stotesbury; Mrs. E. B. McLean casually wore the Hope Diamond to club dinners with her girlfriends. Mrs. O. H. P. Belmont opened up her Marble House in Newport for suffragettes' parties, and stunned a nation by leading the Women's Vote Parade in New York City from Fifty-ninth Street to Washington Square. Alva Belmont may never have walked farther than from her doorstep to a waiting conveyance, but she knew an important gesture when she saw it. "I've ordered a white pleated walking skirt and strong shoes," she simply reassured friends when they said it could not be done.

In more modern times, Brooke Astor carried on with modern flair what many of these women began before her. As head of the Vincent Astor Foundation, and the very model of a modern philanthropist, Brooke Astor has aimed to give away the entirety of her late husband's legacy within the span of her lifetime. New York City, Mrs. Astor decreed, is where the early Astors made their millions; it's here that those rewards should come back. "In thinking over my life, I realize that I am one of the lucky ones," Brooke Astor wrote. "I was taught that life can be a good game if played well and within certain rules."

Mrs. J. Borden Harriman, with her hound in 1910.
Hostess, horse-lover, "Daisy" served as the first president of New York City's preeminent Colony Club for women.

AND STILL THEY RULE THEIR DOMAINS
with charm and presence. In 1976,
Mrs. Alexander Saunderson (born of the Van
Alens and Astors) breakfasts with her husband
in her Santa Barbara bedroom. On the walls are
trompe l'oeil views of Venice, as the city can
only be seen from the Gritti Palace Hotel.

A GRANDE DAME, BY DEFINITION, REGULARLY TAKES A BACK SEAT TO NO ONE. *Right:* Mrs. Tony Hulman in 1980, owner and chairman of the board of the Indianapolis Motor Speedway, host of the Indianapolis 500. Behind the wheel is her daughter, Mari Hulman George. *Above:* In her vintage electric car, Mrs. George W. Merck of Hobe Sound, Florida. For parties at her club, at least in 1974, she'd let valets nowhere near its gleaming fenders. Mrs. Merck parked the car herself.

IN RICHMOND, VIRGINIA, Mrs. John Hill Cronly sits in the ornate Victorian parlor of the Valentine Museum founded by her grandfather, Mann S. Valentine II, in 1898. The tuxedoed men around her, in 1983, are all Valentines.

THESE WERE THE DAYS WHEN WOMEN "DRESSED."
Clockwise, from left: Mrs. Brady Harriman at Bailey's
Beach, Newport, in 1922; Chicago's Mrs. Cyrus Hall
McCormick in white lace for a 1933 at-home garden
party; the unofficial queen of New York City, Grace
Wilson Vanderbilt, in 1919; Mrs. F. Egerton Webb—
who, in *T & C*'s estimate, still reigned in 1913 as
"one of New York's most famous beauties."

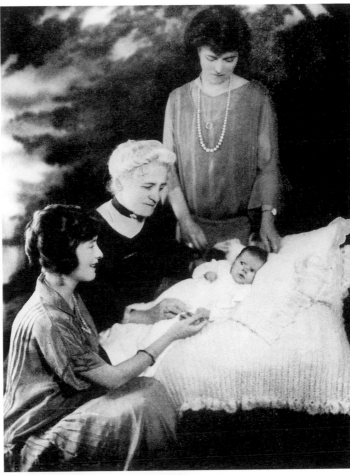

Clockwise from top left: Washington's most important
unofficial hostess, claimed *T & C* of Alice Dows in 1931;
grande dame Mrs. Henry Emerson Hovey poses proudly in
1924 with three generations of her female descendants;
Mrs. John D. Rockefeller, Jr., in 1929, "one of the seven
organizers of the new Museum of Modern Art"; in 1903,
sprightly hatted Mrs. Joseph E. Widener takes in the
Baltimore Horse Show.

PENNSYLVANIA, REPRESENTED EAST AND WEST.
Opposite: In the marbled Heinz Hall,
home of the Pittsburgh Symphony, Drue
Heinz, her husband, H. J. (Jack)
Heinz II, and Jack's aunt, Mrs. Clifford S.
Heinz in 1975. *Above:* Philadelphia
benefactor Mrs. Arthur Pew III, in 1989,
with her grandchildren in the garden of
her summer home.

THE WOMEN OF WASHINGTON.
Above: Mary Gibson Hundley, teacher, Radcliffe honors grad, grande dame of old guard
D.C., in 1975. *Opposite:* Officers of the Daughters of the American Revolution
commemorate, in 1981, the 200th anniversary of the Revolution's closing battle at
Yorktown. *From left:* Anne Dressler, Laura A. Patton, President-General NSDAR
Patricia Shelby, Linda Hatfield, and Catherine E. Anderson.

THE GIVERS.
Left: Oil baroness and art
patron Dominique de Menil
in 1991, before Barnett
Newman's *Now II* (1967)—
one of the modern canvases
in the Menil Collection she
presented to the people of
Houston. *Above:* Mrs. William
K. Vanderbilt, Sr., and
Mrs. Vincent Astor in 1919
arriving home by ocean
liner from war relief work
in France.

In each era, a hostess rises above all others. *Clockwise from near right:* Mrs. Marjorie Merriweather Post, cereal heiress and doyenne of Palm Beach's Mar-A-Largo, in 1971; Mrs. William Woodward, who held forth in the 1960s from her New York City Waldorf Towers apartment; Chicago's legendary Mrs. Potter Palmer, in mourning for her recently deceased mother in 1907, but still a force behind the Charity Ball; her heir to holding the reins of Chicago's social pace, Mrs. William Wood-Prince, in 1978.

STYLE CHANGES, TRADITIONS DO NOT.
New Yorker Mrs. Thomas Hitchcock, widow of the famed social sportsman, takes summer tea in 1986 at the
Canadian lakeside house built by her father, William Larimer Mellon.

163

THE SPORTING SCENE

When you have time and money to spare, recreation quickly becomes an art form—a reason to dress, to travel, to fight fiercely and then turn an opponent into a friend again. It's called sportsmanship. And no one sported harder, through the years, than *Town & Country* people. For polo and golf, for tennis, skiing, squash, and sailing, they bought the requisite ensembles and equipment, took the lessons, formed the clubs, toted away the trophies, then gave the great parties when all was said and done. Some sports, in the States, they virtually invented.

Oh, HOW THEY DRESSED.
Left: Photographer Martin Munkacsi focused on the fundamentals of polo for a 1937 *Town & Country* cover.
Above: Five 1914 "Dianas of the bow" show their stuff on the archery field. *Left to right* are Mrs. Ralph Waldo Emerson, Miss Katherine Green, Mrs. E. E. Trout (winner of the Maid Marion silver arrow), Mrs. R. L. Elmer, and Mrs. John Dunlap, Jr.

Sure, there were the photographs of Yale fencers and Harvard's crew, but the team scene, over 150 years, has never been *Town & Country*'s. Playoff contests and conference titles have passed by, across the seasons, with total indifference. But on the fields of personal combat—the golf links, tennis courts, ski slopes, and steeplechase courses—that's where *Town & Country* offered sports coverage like no other publication. The social sports (polo, shooting, yachting, and sailing) invariably have fared best, each requiring an expanse of land or sea, largesse, and added hands to adequately support it. Animals figure importantly: they're raised, raced, ridden, taken into the fields, or bred for future generations with heartbreaking devotion. Show dogs, field dogs, horses that are jumpers or highsteppers—all find their place and personality on *T & C* pages.

Where else could a reader learn about the private golf course that John D. Rockefeller laid out for himself in 1898 at Pocantico Hills? Or the day Andrew Carnegie finally broke par on the fifth hole of St. Andrew's Golf Club in Westchester? What about the Cretan antiquity that graced the bottom of the pool on Aristotle Onassis' floating estate?

Readers have watched mogul Frank Jay Gould attack at court tennis, gone skiing at Gstaad with J. Kenneth Galbraith, and flown across polo fields with the ever elegant Jock Whitney. *T & C* took subscribers camping in the Rockies with Teddy Roosevelt and sons, and let them take aim with bow and arrow alongside Mrs. Ralph Waldo Emerson. In 1907, Grover Cleveland kindly supplied fishing tips to *Town & Country*'s readers. The former President scorned trolling and fly casting; he was firmly of the school of live bait. Best of all, Cleveland claimed, was the pleasure provided by landing a black bass— "more uncertain, whimsical and wary in biting, and more strong, resolute and resourceful when hooked than any other fish." Cleveland might as well have been talking about *Town & Country*'s sports-loving women and men.

TUXEDO PARK RESIDENTS
Mr. L. J. Hunt and Mrs. H. H. Rogers, Jr., take to the ice in 1912.

THE PACE CHANGES.
In 1983, sailors duel for the
America's Cup in twelve-meter
yachts. Costing then about
$350,000 to build, the
competing sloops weighed
56,000 pounds; their masts
rose eighty-eight feet above
the water.

THE GUYS MADE GOLF
THE SPORT IT IS.
From left: In 1927,
sportswriter Walter
Trumbull; H. J. Whigham,
national amateur champion
in 1896 and 1897 and for
twenty-five years editor of
Town & Country; Charles
Blair Macdonald, 1895
amateur champion and
Whigham's father-in-law.
Architect John W. Cross
completes the foursome.

THE SOCIAL SIDE OF
RACQUET SPORTS.
Opposite: French beauty and
tennis star Florence La Caze
(famed, too, for being the third
wife of American spendthrift
Frank Jay Gould) plays an
exhibition match in the 1920s.
This page: 1930s national
champions James Van Alen (*top
and bottom*) and Ogden Phipps
show how court tennis is played.

RIDING OUT.
The Brandywine Valley is home
turf to Wyeths and du Ponts,
and Mr. Stewart's Cheshire
Foxhounds—an American hunt
that dates back to 1912.

FOR THE LOVE OF A HORSE. *Clockwise from left:* Sandra Payson set for riding in 1948; equestrienne twins Laura and Nancy Lee and Betsy Ann Lewis, 1940; horsewoman Vera Cravath, a Piping Rock winner in 1911, sitting sidesaddle. *Opposite:* Sonny and Mary Lou Whitney check out the crop of yearlings on their Kentucky farm in 1959.

A DARE AND A PRAYER.

Above: On the polo fields of Palm Beach in 1980. *Opposite, from top:* Mrs. Edwin H. Thompkins, Miss Marcia Meigs, Mrs. Dorothy O'Connor, and Mrs. George Snowden, all set to splash into the pool at Bermuda's Castle Harbour Hotel in 1933.

THE BOYS OF SUMMER,
SPRING (AND FALL).
Above: R. J. Collier at bat,
Mr. Payne Whitney catching
in 1911. *Left:* Alexander
Woolcott battles at croquet in
1938 at Vermont's Neshobe
Island Club. *Opposite: (below)*
The Taft School scrimmages in
1933; *(above)* a champion in
the making—Tommy Tailer in
1927. At just fourteen, said
T & C, "No young player has
ever showed greater promise."

On the hunt.
Clockwise, from top left:
Lord Ashburton and
Paul A. Curtis at the 1933
Labrador Retriever Club's
field trial; in 1932, sisters
Mrs. Donald Frothingham and
Miss Georgette Delafield go
duck shooting in Connecticut;
ex-President Grover
Cleveland takes aim in 1907.
Opposite: "Speed and style are
the keys to winning field
trials," said kennel owner
Mrs. Edward Carey, in 1991.
"A retriever must have
enthusiasm!"

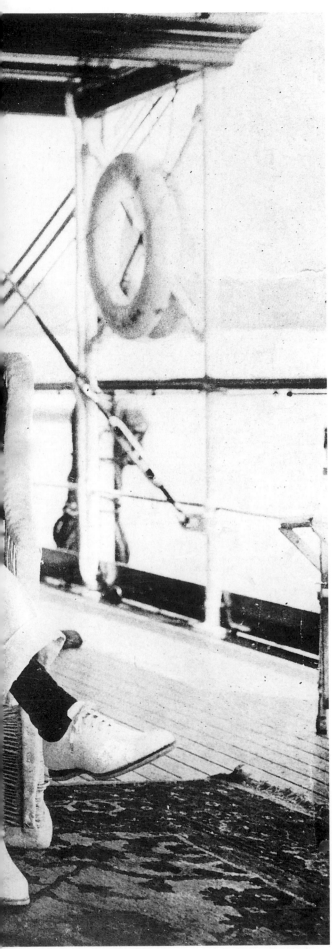

THE WAY OF A SAILOR.
Left: Commodore Cornelius
Vanderbilt III and Fleet
Captain Grenville Kane of the
1907 New York Yacht Club.
Above: Arthur Lee Kinsolving,
Jr., sixty years later.

It's all in the breeding.
From the paddocks and
pristinely groomed land of
Kentucky's famed Calumet
Farm (here, in 1978)
have come star Thoroughbreds
Citation and Man O' War.
Society always loves a winner.

SOME SPORTS, BY THEIR VERY NATURE, REQUIRE ACREAGE, land to roam and ride. *Opposite:* A day's shooting at South Carolina's Medway Plantation—as photographer Toni Frissell saw it in 1949. *Right:* Frank Iglehart and Redmond C. Stewart, Jr., at hounds in 1934; *below,* with a guide, Jay Gould and daughter Anne hit the trail in 1931.

Socio-intellectual sports. William F. Buckley, Jr., and John Kenneth Galbraith take a seat in Gstaad, Switzerland, in 1977. Why Gstaad? "It's the one place where I can look at the telephone and want it to ring," said Galbraith.

BORN AND BRED BEAUTIES

Before there were Hollywood starlets, Olympic sports stars, talk show queens, and supermodels—centuries before MTV—Americans looked to a different sort of icon, and she was a woman famed simply for the quality of her beauty. She was photographed at El Morocco, at the races, on her way to Europe aboard the *Queen Mary*. Blessed with money and more-than-enough breeding, she made news in any given season simply with the clothes she wore. Sometimes, she loaned her glorious face to *Town & Country*'s covers.

IMAGES OF ACKNOWLEDGED BEAUTY.

Above: Grace of Monaco, America's own princess, untouchably regal in 1965. *Left:* "Babe," Mrs. William Paley, photographed in 1957 by Richard Avedon. "I think true beauty is made, not born," suggested Avedon, at the time. "Beauty is perhaps always a kind of becoming."

Sure, the magazine played favorites. And in any era, certain women turned up with regularity. In the innocence of America before the Great War, no one composed a picture quite like Consuelo Vanderbilt. As the Duchess of Marlborough, she arrayed her long skirts and her children about her with grace and glory. Mrs. William Rhinelander Stewart, doyenne of New York society for two decades from the 1930s, shone from her earliest childhood years. Then there were the beautiful blondes, Philadelphia's Grace Kelly and New York's famous C-Z. Pale, patrician, made for a cinched-waist and bare-shouldered dress, C-Z Guest was truly memorable. Truman Capote was introduced to her by Cecil Beaton on the opening night of Broadway's *My Fair Lady*. Some twenty years later he remembered the occasion clearly—and what C-Z had on that night: "A Mainbocher column of white crepe de Chine. No jewelry, not much makeup; just *blanc de blanc* perfection."

Accepted notions of what's lovely—and exactly who's lovely—change noticeably through the years. *Town & Country*'s turn-of-the-century virgins in white batiste would blanch at the vision of Isabella Rossellini, curled up and barefoot on the floor, in sweater and trousers. By the late 1960s, *T & C*'s precisely groomed ladies had moved outdoors, and had their hair windblown. They posed on the ski slopes or muscling a rowboat. The legendary black-and-white studio images composed by Hoyningen-Huene and Baron de Meyer have, in later days, been reframed with bright color, sun, movement, and a hint of sex. Beauty now is less form than function.

But perhaps the most appealing side to *Town & Country*'s acknowledged beauties, through 150 years, is their total lack of facts that are "up-close and personal." They may have deigned to appear in Valentino, Norman Norell, Madame Grès, Charles James, or Jean Patou, thereby granting those designers their unspoken approval, but these women did it with aplomb. They never opened up their closets to be rummaged through; they offered no exercise routines or cosmetic secrets. They dined, they danced, they dressed to great effect. They offered their features, their faces, their grace—with style, yes, but also with quiet.

Baron de meyer's
famous portrait of Mrs. Philip M. Lydig, as it ran in *Town & Country* in 1913.

THEY WERE VISIBLY LADIES, FOR ANY AGE.

Opposite: Mrs. Patrick Guinness in white piqué by Jean Patou, photographed in Paris, 1957. *Above:* In 1911, Miss Agnes Leroy Edgar was a post-deb and "one of the most popular young women." *T & C* thoughtfully provided her New York address in its accompanying caption.

Out of the drawing rooms and into the sun.
Opposite: Marina Rust, granddaughter of Marshall Field III and a
published novelist at 27, in 1993. *Above:* Jeannine and Serena Rhinelander
cast off from Newport in 1972. *T & C* was especially fond of the sisters'
"sterling American good looks."

THE WORLD'S A STAGE.

Above: Miss Katharine Price Collier, photographed by Baron de Meyer in 1916. To raise funds for scholarships, she and her sister took the role of sea nymphs in a pageant given by the Society of Beaux Arts Architects. *Opposite:* In 1962, Dina Merrill may have starred in Hollywood family comedies, but as Marjorie Merriweather Post's daughter she knew all about white gloves.

It all begins with a great background. *Far right:* Mrs. Alfred G. Vanderbilt in 1962 white Mainbocher. *Right:* Mrs. Winston F. C. Guest, dressed for 1959. Explained friend Truman Capote, of the famous "C-Z": "Actually, her name is Lucy; but the only person who calls her that is her husband." Her hair, said Truman, was "paler than Dom Perignon."

Clockwise from left: Sarah Sherman Wiborg, at the time of her engagement to Gerald Murphy in 1915. By the 1920s, the Murphys were Scott Fitzgerald's favorite symbols of "living well." In 1936, Patricia Havens-Monteagle wed Richard Palmer Smart, heir to a Hawaiian sugar plantation. Lucille Brokaw debuted four years earlier, reported *T & C,* at a dance given by her godmother, "Princess Henry XXXIII of Reuss." Miss Elinor Patterson, of Chicago, headed to Los Angeles to become an actress. In 1927, she "at the last report was sunning herself as a private resident in Beverly Hills, California."

From top left: In 1929, Lily Cushing was "to be wed at Trinity Church, Newport." Mrs. Lydig Hoyt, in 1921, stood as "one of the most decorative figures in society." The fabled Mrs. William Rhinelander Stewart was simply, said *T & C* in 1946, "a belle in any time." Mary Ridgely Carter, in 1930, spent "the greater part of her time running over to Paris."

S**OME INSTINCTIVELY KNEW ABOUT GLAMOUR.**
Above: Mary Elizabeth Altemus, in 1930, a horsewoman,
a charmer, the announced wife-to-be of John Hay Whitney.
Opposite: In 1932, Dorothy Quimby Paine was newly returned
home with the mysteries she learned while traveling in Morocco.

Even young women of the nicest families became John Powers models in 1939. *Right:* Mrs. Roger Vasselais, born Joan Hamilton, had a five-year-old blond-headed, black-eyed son, a way with fetching poses, and fame as one of Saks Fifth Avenue's most important mannequins. Hoyningen-Huene made the photograph.

They carried their tiaras gracefully.
Opposite: The exquisite Consuelo Vanderbilt, in 1911, reigned as
the Duchess of Marlborough. *Above:* In England in 1921 the
former Nancy Langhorne from Virginia was a member of
Parliament, one of London's ruling hostesses, and Lady Astor.

THEY DRESSED, THEY DINED, THEY ALL MODELED.

Above: Patsy, of the publishing Pulitzers, in 1949, the year of her wedding to David Bartlett. For *T & C,* she stepped out in pink satin and black net. *Opposite:* Mrs. R. M. Warren, in 1953, made the perfect young matron, ready for dinner-dancing in red silk with "a butterfly back bow."

"COOL LIGHTS AND WARM SHADOWS"
rhapsodized *T & C* in 1931 over Baron de Meyer's image *(opposite)* of Miss Marjorie
Curtis. *Above:* The Misses Natalie and Mimi Kountze, photographed
by Lee Miller in 1933. The sisters seem somewhat less than ecstatic. Their
engagements were announced just a week apart that season.

LADIES COULD ALSO PLAY COME-HITHER.
Above: Mrs. Amory S. Carhart, Jr., born Lucile Harris,
here in 1948. *Opposite:* Mrs. Howard Hawks, 1961.
Strong, individual, they gave high-style blood and substance.

THE LOOK BECAME EASIER, MORE NATURAL, VISIBLY YOUNGER.
Above: Ballet student and granddaughter of a U.S. senator,
Tripler Pell charms in 1988. *Opposite:* India Hicks, in 1995.
Daughter of English interior designer David Hicks, she,
too, had a famous grandfather. He was Mountbatten.

ARTS AND BEYOND

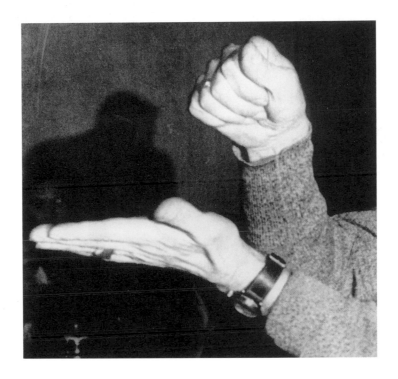

S hould they be looking for some sophisti-
cation, *Town & Country* explained to its readers in 1933 exactly what constituted the "Smart
Set": "The nucleus is always a few people so rich that they shine," wrote then-Managing
Editor J. Bryan, III. "To these is added a lump of foreign artists and noblemen, then a
columnist or a playwright; some lovely hard-shelled debutante; a bathed politician; a gentleman rider; and an actress who does not get too abominably drunk."

M AESTRO ARTURO TOSCANINI
played outdoors (*left*) with his granddaughter, Sonia Horowitz, in 1954. *Above:* Music was made in 1957– most emphatically,
assisted by the hand gestures of composer/conductor Igor Stravinsky.

Modern-day Michelangelos might not be thrilled with the particular grouping, nor a squeaky-clean politico with the dipsomaniac. But society, in truth, has always loved its artists: the ones who paint them, like Whistler or Warhol; the ones who play with them, like Salvador Dalí, Noel Coward, or Maria Callas. Truman Capote was drawn to the very social dames like a hungry boy to a batch of warm cookies. Mary Cassatt and Edith Wharton, by virtue of their very proper births, held a special place in the pages of *Town & Country*. Boston Lowells and Adamses were, as old-time Yankees, readily taken at their word.

The rich and the famous may never fully trust each other, but they have plenty in common. For starters, they both love a great bash. Writers, displaced painters, and musicians turn up in intriguing places: Noel Coward and Cole Porter lounging on a Venetian beach in the 1920s; Henri Matisse, after judging a 1930s art competition, sailing home on the *Ile-de-France*. Debut tours, farewell tours, talking tours—by the Ballet Russe or Eleanora Duse, William Butler Yeats or Rudolf Nureyev—made *T & C* news. Oscar Wilde's ruffled shirts, kid gloves, and knee britches among the American philistines provided lines of copy at the turn of the century.

Americans expect even their Great Talents to be human; Maestro Toscanini might wear a tailcoat and striped trousers, but he played hide-and-seek with a young granddaughter around a big tree like any lesser man. In the 1950s *Town & Country* ran a regular Happy Birthday series of articles: "Happy Birthday, dear Robert Frost," and another month, "Dear Evelyn Waugh." V. S. Pritchett wrote Waugh's birthday ode; Gertie Lawrence sent her annual wishes to Noel Coward. Bing publicly thanked God for Irving Berlin. And, suddenly, well, you hoped they all got loads of great presents.

THEY WERE ARTISTS,
but they were also individuals with noticeable style—and frailties.
Opposite: F. Scott and Zelda Fitzgerald, as they appeared in *Town & Country* in 1923.

On the Lido, in 1926,
the importance of being idle.
At far left is Noel Coward;
extreme right, Cole Porter.
Between them are Jack
Wilson, Miss Dicky Fellowes-
Gordon, and young George
Abdy, son of Sir Richard and
Lady Abdy.

D<small>ANCE MASTERS.</small>
Opposite: Anna Pavlova, in
1913, on her farewell
American tour.
Above: George Balanchine
focuses on a score at a 1952
New York City Ballet
rehearsal.

P<small>EACE AND WAR</small>.

Above: In 1907, Count Leo Tolstoy meets with his foreign literary representative, Captain Vladimir Tchertkoff. *Opposite:* In 1953, at Bimini, Ernest Hemingway and Michael Lerner congratulate themselves on each landing a pair of 400-pound marlins. Hemingway was a notable deep-sea man. "His dictum," reported *T & C*, "was to fight every fish as hard as possible without breaking the rod, the line, or the fisherman."

Opposite: IN 1916, Serge Diaghilev arrived in New York with his touring Ballet Russe company of dancers. *Right:* In 1930, Pablo Picasso had two New York shows. "His drawings are in a class by themselves," said *T & C,* "and as far as buying them goes, it is a class more difficult to enter every day." Photograph by Man Ray. *Below right:* Thomas Mann and his daughter enjoyed the slopes at St. Moritz in 1932. *Below left:* Anatole France, in 1920, was simply "a leader among French litterateurs."

Clockwise from right: Aldous Huxley and his son Mathew, in 1931; the author of *Six Characters in Search of an Author,* Luigi Pirandello; Claude Monet, at age 84 in 1924. *Opposite:* In 1923, Captain Joseph Conrad steamed up New York harbor on his first visit there. "He much prefers to be known," explained *T & C* familiarly, "by his nautical title."

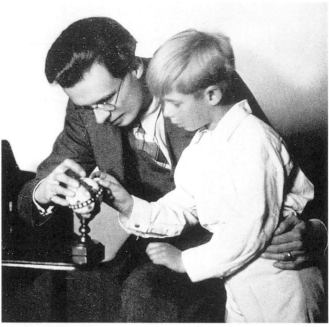

A PRIDE OF LIONS
FROM THE BRITISH ISLES.
Standing, from left:
G. K. Chesterton, James
Stephens, Lennox Robinson.
Seated: W. B. Yeats (in silk hat),
Compton Mackenzie,
Augustus John,
and Sir Edwin Lutyens.

S OME ARTISTS WERE
ALSO GREAT LADIES.
Clockwise from right: Mrs. Edith
Wharton, in 1902; diva Fritzi
Scheff, star of the Knickerbocker
Theater, in 1908; Signora
Eleanora Duse, in 1902,
acting in a D'Annunzio drama.
Opposite: "Impeccable,
immaculate, gleaming" is how an
aging Colette looked to *T & C* in
1953. Mostly bed-bound with
arthritis, this self-proclaimed
"genuinely womanly writer"
could still show a visitor a thing
or two. Beneath the sheets, her
toenails were painted bright,
bright red.

237

TWO FOR THE SHOW.
Left: "She is endowed with that rare quality that can make people feel at least happy, at best hysterical, merely by her appearance on a stage." She was Beatrice Lillie, charming everyone in 1952. *Above:* In 1954, *Town & Country* asked Bing Crosby for a birthday toast to composer Irving Berlin. To the man who gave him, among other goodies, a song called "White Christmas," Bing proclaimed, "Every singer, every musician, everyone who ever performed or sang your wonderful songs must on your day say, 'Thank God for Irving Berlin.' I know I do."

Clockwise from top left: In 1930, Henri Matisse headed home from America on the *Ile-de-France;* Dr. Thomas Hardy, D.L., showed his honors at Oxford in 1920; on the Left Bank, e.e. cummings talked across a cafe table to his wife, model Marian Morehouse; Erich Maria Remarque's *"All Quiet on the Western Front* had already sold three-and-a-half million copies," *T & C* reported somewhat skeptically, in 1931, "if the publishers are to be believed."

Clockwise from top left:

W. Somerset Maugham in the gardens of Shepherd's Hotel, Cairo, in 1930; William Butler Yeats, in 1920 on a poem-reading tour of America; humorist P. G. Wodehouse in 1932 took on Hollywood; in 1927, *T & C* claimed Jean Cocteau was "author, poet, musician, and artist, one of the most brilliant and versatile of the younger group in France."

THE COMPANY THEY KEEP.
Opposite, from bottom:
Photographer Man Ray, his
pupil Lee Miller, Mr. and Mrs.
Max Ernst. In 1932, the
Surrealists were exhibiting in
New York City. *Above:* In
mid-twenties Paris, three
groundbreaking literary
men—Ford Madox Ford,
James Joyce, and poet
Ezra Pound.

THEY SAW AN AMERICA THAT WAS DIFFERENT.

Opposite: Eugene O'Neill, surrounded by the African masks he collected. In 1946, his *The Iceman Cometh* and *A Moon for the Misbegotten* both opened. *Above:* In 1902, Mark Twain was America's dearly beloved. Twain took to winter spas for his health; small-town society turned out the invitations.

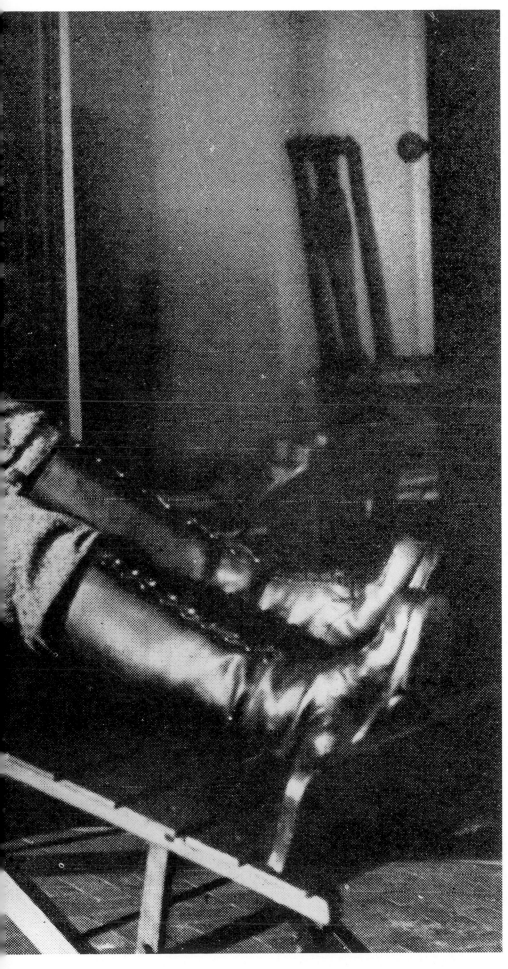

His tweeds were tailored, his boots were polished, his beard neatly trimmed— and George Bernard Shaw looked, in 1922, every inch the country gentleman. Not true, said *Town & Country*. He "posed in typically careless fashion at his home at Ayot St. Lawrence, Herts., England."

FOR RICHER, FOR POORER

A meeting, a merger, a marvelous party to close off the deal: what could be better than a very social marriage? Weddings are so wonderfully predictable, so filled with promise, crafted with age-old rituals and a reassuring cast of characters in expected roles—not-so-blushing brides, awkward grooms, aspiring in-laws, embarrassing uncles with a taste for vodka, harassed fathers who, only half-begrudgingly, mortgage the estate to pick up the whopping bill. Beneath it all is a subtext of hopes fulfilled or quietly shelved, of youthful exuberance, and, at last, publicly sanctioned sex. Beneath the yards of tulle, there's invariably a great tale to tell.

Living arrangements, these days, have changed. And, except perhaps in the Deep

M RS. EARL F. T. SMITH, BORN CONSUELO VANDERBILT
(left) in her 1926 bridal portrait by Steichen, reprinted with permission of Joanna T. Steichen. *Above:* By 1970, bride Ferrell Barfield Page (Foxcroft, Radcliffe) and groom W. Chichester McLean III were both in training at Morgan Guaranty Trust.

South, brides and grooms are more often in their thirties than their post-teen years. The rites they marry by, though, have remained constant. And for 150 years, *Town & Country* has detailed the menus of the wedding breakfasts, counted the tents, assessed the bride's portion and the gifts of nearly useless sterling serving pieces proudly arrayed in the dining room of the girl's parents. In 1903, when May Goelet married the Duke of Roxburghe at St. Thomas's Church in New York, the magazine faithfully reported on the "Marie Antoinette attire" of the bridesmaids and the "frenzied excitement" of the Fifth Avenue crowds. Most foreign aristocrats marrying young American heiresses in the new century fared even less well, generally characterized as idle, avaricious, overly eager, and, worst of all, of puny physique compared with strapping Americans.

A new generation of news photographers regularly supplied the record of "important nuptials" throughout the 1920s and 1930s; proper brides in later years were formally photographed by Bachrach or Jay Te Winburn. Today, the proceedings, say clergymen, more often than not go on videotape, and a host of second marriages fill small chapels rather than spill over into cathedral aisles. But the great snapshots live on. In 1987, the magazine, only half-facetiously, told readers "How to Get Your Picture in *Town & Country*." ("Informal glossies," nothing older than a few months, a self-addressed stamped envelope for returns, no bribes of champagne or chocolates accepted.)

In the 1990s, satin dresses may be by New York's Vera Wang, not Worth of Paris, but they require as much time, attention, and cold cash invested as they did at the turn of the century. Tiny child attendants still gamely struggle under the weight of unaccustomed responsibility and uncomfortable suitings. Grooms wander a bit aimlessly. And mothers, well, they keep on sobbing. In 1938, the magazine lamented what little role the mother-of-the-bride was given at the big event. "Today, a maternal parent's part is often as not confined to weeping softly in the front pew in Henri Bendel's handsomest beige crepe." Almost sixty years later, that mother-in-law-to-be may hire a wedding planner, but she's still settling correctly for that beige crepe dress. After all, it's her daughter's day. And if she's lucky, there will be someone there to tell everyone all about it.

Society changes, ceremony doesn't.
Opposite: Contessina Teresa Martini Marescotti marries American John Oliver Crane in 1929 Rome.

WHAT A WONDERFUL EXCUSE FOR A PARTY.
In 1933, a hunt breakfast at Far Hills's Ripplebrook
Farm celebrates the marriage of Eleanor Schley
to Webster Todd. In 1992, the couple's daughter,
Christine Todd Whitman, became governor
of New Jersey.

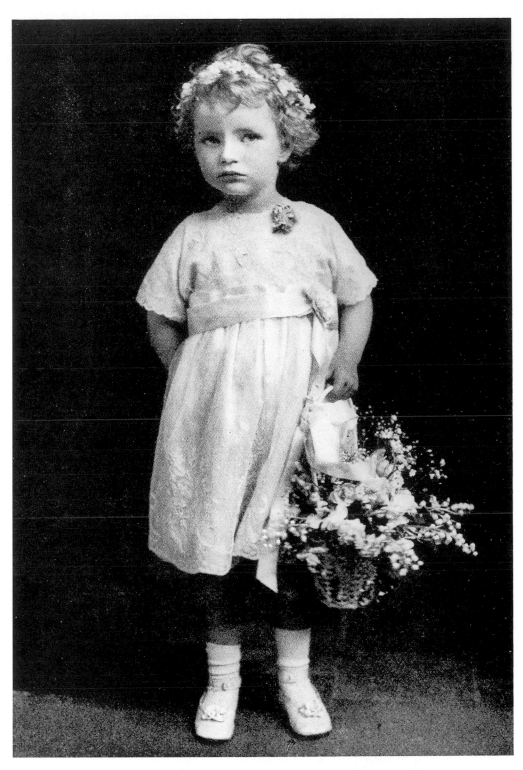

THE LITTLEST BRIDES AND GROOMS.
They dress in white, lug flowers or a bridal
train, and regret the resulting photographs in
later life—it's the lot of flower girls and pages.
Opposite: In 1923, *Town & Country* told its readers
that the charming outfits of Miss Kathleen
Martyn and her young attendants could be
found at Best & Co. *Above:* Even in 1915,
Doris Duke was solemnly suspicious
of press attention.

THE WOMEN WORE WHITE.
Looking down demurely, and hoisting a greenhouse-worth of blooms in their bridal bouquets, they married publicly, proudly, sometimes even wisely. *Above:* In 1907, the new Mrs. Ulysses S. Grant. The daughter of Secretary of State Elihu Root chose the grandson of a former president. *Above, left:* Ethel Roosevelt on her 1913 wedding day with her father, Theodore. *Left:* Betsey Cushing of Brookline, Massachusetts, weds another president's son, James Roosevelt.

Above: Carlotta Busch at her 1948 Grant's Farm, St. Louis, wedding to second cousin John Flanigan. Both were great-grandchildren of the St. Louis beer baron. World War I–era bride, *above right,* Mrs. George Humphreys from Morristown, New Jersey; *right,* Chicagoan Mrs. William B. Mann, with Aline Manierre, her sister and attendant.

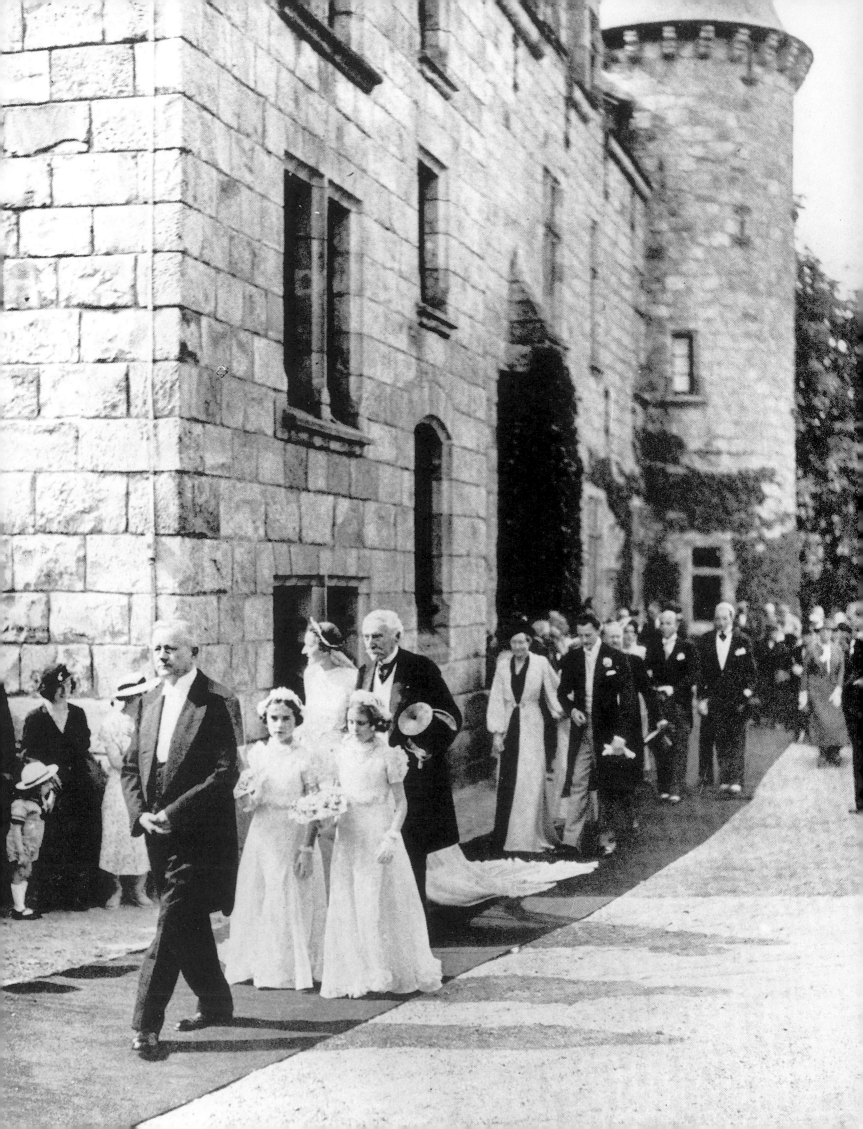

FORM FOLLOWS FAMILIES.
Above: The bride, Averell Adelaide Ross, hailed from Ardmore, Pa.; her 1932 groom was
Philadelphia-bred Edmond du Pont. *Opposite:* At the Château du Marais, the country house of the
bride's mother, Helen Violette de Talleyrand Périgord weds Count James de Pourtales.
The maiden name of the mother of the titled bride was simply Anna Gould.

MARRIAGE TIMES AREN'T
MOMENTS TO BE MODEST.
At the 1910 merger
of Marjorie Gould to
A.J. Drexel, Jr., seventeen
attendants line up at
the Gould family's Fifth
Avenue residence.

PRIVATE MOMENTS, PUBLIC STAGES.
Above: Tiny Christina
Perpignano and Emily Cole
were 1993 flower girls at the
executive mansion reception
of then New York governor
Mario Cuomo's daughter,
Madeline, to Brian John
O'Donoghue. *Opposite:*
Martha Sharp ("Sunny")
Crawford at her first
marriage, in 1957, to Prince
Alfred von Auersperg.

Above: A wedding breakfast toast to Virginia Tucker Kent and Cummins Catherwood at Bryn Mawr, Pa., in 1935. *Above right:* Hundreds of tables filled the tented gardens of the five-square-mile Duke's Farms estate in Somerville, New Jersey. The occasion was Mary L. Duke tying up, in 1915, with A. J. Biddle, Jr. *Right:* Guests kick up their heels at the July 4, 1914, marriage of Emily Randolph to Philip Stevenson at Wildfield Farm, Narragansett Pier, Rhode Island.

ALWAYS THERE WAS THE CHANCE
FOR A FASHION STATEMENT.
The message, even deep in the Great
Depression, could be anything from
nunlike to Paris couture. *Opposite:* Mrs.
Allan A. Ryan, Jr., turned out for
her 1929 Washington, D.C., wedding.
Above: Mrs. Dorland Doyle (née Pauline
Munn) at her mother's St.-Jean-Cap-
Ferrat villa. The bride's white
crepe satin gown in 1931 was from
Worth in Paris; ditto those of her
bridesmaids—"femininely fluffy
in white organdy."

267

AT HAMMERSMITH FARM, in 1953, there was beauty, there was laughter, there was an abundance of great teeth. With Jacqueline and John F. Kennedy *(in rear from left):* Michael Canfield, Charles Bartlett, Paul Fay, Edward Kennedy, Lem Billings, Joseph Gargan, Sargent Shriver, Robert Kennedy, James Reed, and Charles Spalding. *Front row, from left:* Yusha Auchincloss III, George Smathers, Torbert MacDonald, Ben Smith. Photograph by Toni Frissell.

And so it ends and reality of varying kinds begins. *Opposite:* Groom John Gefaell in 1940 parts from his dapper men. *Left:* Bridesmaids reach for a bride's bouquet tossed from the New York Colony Club balcony in 1938. Brides still repeat the gesture there today.

PORTRAITS

by Louis Auchincloss

In our century, photographers have learned to cover every aspect of the human condition, from the coronation of a monarch or a moon landing to the grisliest details of poverty and war. But before the age of the camera, we had only the artist to represent us, and the artist tended to draw, paint, or sculpt the images of those who paid him. History is chiefly illustrated in the portraits of the upper class. When I think of Tudor days, the pale set features of Holbein's sitters bring alive to me a court where men and women gambled with death to obtain power. In the romantic countenances of Charles I's cavaliers, I read the impending doom of a chivalrous order. Turning the pages of this wonderful volume, I recognize that *Town & Country* is fulfilling the old role of the court illustrator of fashion. And in studying fashion, we may penetrate to some important aspects of the era that defined what fashion was and is.

Even Napoleon, who at the height of his power still cultivated the aristocrats of the *ancien régime,* maintained that a successful government must always come to terms with fashion.

The question is often raised: is there an American aristocracy? In Europe, the term has always been associated with wealth and power derived from land—land that was both

Social historian, observer of mores and manners, Old Guard attorney, author of more than fifty books, Louis Auchincloss has known the people on these pages firsthand. He first contributed his tale "The Ambassadress" to *Town & Country* in 1950. At right, in 1987, he's in his beloved Museum of the City of New York—where he acted for many years as president.

rural and inherited, whereas wealth originating in commerce was indelibly tainted. An aristocrat could make up for diminished rents by marrying the daughter of a money-lender, his title obliterating her usurious origin, but he would never take a seat behind the counter himself. In America, only the great planters of our antebellum South could validly claim to have been aristocrats. The makers and heirs of our commercial fortunes bear the permanent stamp of the urban bourgeoisie. It is for them that we have added the qualification "upper" to "middle class."

But the term doesn't mean that its members haven't aspired at least to resemble those of the higher order. A hankering for the things least connected with the marketplace is a prime characteristic of the heirs of the great American capitalists. They go in for wide country domains and splendid country houses reminiscent of the proud seats of landed peers, for the sports of old: hunting, shooting and polo, games emulating the valor of more lethal contests, when physical courage was the indispensable mark of the knight. Casual clothes, ease of manner, disdain of penny-pinching, the cultivation of farms and gardens, the love of animals, the identification of oneself with healthy pursuits, "real things," "natural things"— all these go into the making of the American "aristocrat."

Laurance and Mary Rockefeller, leaning on a fence before a barn, in country boots and jeans, and with light brown sweaters loosely tied around their necks, smilingly radiate their congeniality with a rustic scene far removed from oil or philanthropy. Nelson's granddaughters, seated on rocks at Maine's picturesque, mountain-lined Jordan Pond, seem equally integrated with the sylvan scene. The visions of sport are as beautiful as those of nature, and evocative of risk and daring. We recall the line in *The Philadelphia Story:* "What is prettier than the sight of the privileged classes enjoying their privileges?"

Country clothes need not, however, be always casual. Not anyway in spas and stables. Anthony J. Drexel in a black fedora, white trousers, and gleaming footwear, one hand resting in lordly fashion on the handle of his umbrella, has the air of a gentleman of the 1930s who is still not afraid to be stylish.

The social-climbing inside trader in the film *Wall Street,* seeking the prestige of membership on the board of the Bronx Zoo, remarks that WASPs don't like people, but they "sure as hell like animals." And surely nothing is stronger in England or America than the devotion of the upper classes to horses and dogs. One might even say that the greatest beauty in rural playgrounds is found in horse territory and that the heirs of leisure are at their most picturesque as equestrians. When the hounds join the riders, as in a fox hunt, it is indeed a glorious sight.

I recall in my law school days at the University of Virginia how I pined to join the Charlottesville hunt, but a fellow student had missed a term because of a bad fall, and I thought I owed to my father not to take the risk. But watching the thrilling plunge and dash of the hunt, I could understand those who claimed there was no pleasure in sport quite like it. Today in England there are people who throw themselves in front of the riders to stop the fun, and no doubt it is cruel to terrify poor foxes, but I still wonder if it can be right to arrest so splendid and long enduring a sport.

If we move back in time to the founders of the feast—"robber barons" to the radical, but to the Tory (in the phrase of an old-time eulogist) "men puffed with divine greed"— we are faced with images that are less posed, taken perhaps against the vociferously stated objection of the subject. The first John Pierpont Morgan certainly does not see us, nor does he want to, as he swings by with his wife in a victoria, affording a rare glimpse of the disfigured nose that was his bitter cross. Andrew Carnegie, standing impassive but patient, in the garden of his vast Manhattan mansion, has made no effort to adjust himself for the benefit of the picture. It is the same with John D. Rockefeller, Sr., and Andrew Mellon: these men have no need to dress up, to smile, to say "cheese," to apologize for their millions by offering us a pretty or even an interesting picture. They are what they have made themselves, and that should be enough for us. It is certainly enough for them. Mr. Morgan was known, on at least one occasion, outside the Metropolitan Opera House, to have raised his cane in a violently threatening gesture toward an intrusive cameraman.

All this, however, was to change. Subsequent generations of tycoons, if they continued like William Henry Vanderbilt to damn the public, were careful to do so in selected company or under their breath. Theodore Roosevelt, a worse "traitor to his class" than his fifth cousin of a later era, for he was a Republican, had made trust-busting almost a national sport. It was better now to placate a potentially truculent majority, and better, too, for business and sales, not to shake the mailed fists.

Donald W. Douglas, his eyes averted to the distance in a General MacArthur gaze, stands tall and strong beneath a propeller of one of his great aircraft. Malcolm Forbes, with a foxy grin, holds up a million-dollar Fabergé Easter egg for our delectation. J. Paul Getty has even dressed up for his portrait, in a light sport coat and tan sweater designed to blend with the paneled wall of his library and the flesh colors in the Renaissance painting behind him. His brow is pricked in the slight frown of the great collector to whom these things are always serious.

Money has done much for the beautification of rural areas (perhaps the ultimate example is the sweeping panorama of the paddocks of Calumet Farm in Kentucky, fenced in with such marvelous geometric precision). But the city, after all, was the source of revenue and remained the principal residence for those who worked, and at least a winter one for those who played. Even the most rustic of English peers accorded his womenfolk, however grumblingly, a season in London during June and July.

Before World War I, urban entertainment in America was largely confined to the Beaux Arts mansions lining the main boulevards, in which it would not have been seemly for the guests to be photographed. But when society embraced the virtue-in-hedonism artifice of the charity ball, only the grand ballrooms of major hotels could accommodate the crowds. Escape from the camera was no longer possible or even desirable—the advertisement of good works spawned others. And how many beautiful women, dressed by Dior or Givenchy and engaged in philanthropic endeavor, would object to a little flattering publicity?

Yet there is often a sniping side in our reaction to snapshots of well-attired people hilariously enjoying an evening party. All those grins and roars of laughter, all those funny faces and clowning—were they really having that good a time? Could anyone? Wasn't the dance floor too crowded? And the service slow? And there was always the inevitable, the indefatigable Elsa Maxwell presiding over the revelry, a stout female Silenus whose credo was that there was no law of diminishing returns, that two parties a night were twice the fun of one, and three, three times better.

But Elsa was only a *dame d'honneur* in this brave new world. Its real leaders were the Windsors: a king, degraded and aimless, who had shed his crown for love, and the stony-willed Duchess, who had substituted for him the tinsel crown of fashion. They were like the puppet monarchs in a carnival, hailed at night and forgotten in the morning by men who returned to the "real world" of downtown.

Not all charity balls, by any means, were tedious. Too much depended on the revenue derived. I recall a wonderful party that purported to duplicate the 1860 ball for the Prince of Wales in the old Academy of Music, where the guests turned up in an impressive display of crinolines and mutton-chop whiskers. And one where a supposedly medieval meal was served in the cloisters of the Cloisters Museum. I heard Mrs. August Belmont's warning to the committee: "I hope there's no nonsense about the cocktails."

If one turns to the photographs of some of the splendid women who attended these festivals—Mrs. W. Palmer Dixon, Mrs. Lewis Preston, Marie M. McKim, Mme Toulgouat—one perhaps finds the best excuse for these entertainments. These pictures seem to have supplied their viewers with the same satisfaction as did the vended postcards in late-nineteenth-century London of such famous beauties as Lillie Langtry or Lady Randolph Churchill, or Alexandra, Princess of Wales.

A social phenomenon even more curious than the charity ball was the development, in the 1920s and 1930s, of the debutante party. This was originally designed by the parents of a seventeen- or eighteen-year-old daughter as the means for introducing her formally to their society, old and young, to indicate that she was "out" in the world of adults. In time, this "coming out" party evolved into a dance (sometimes for those of limited means, merely tea), primarily for one's daughter's debutante friends and eligible bachelors, plus a few relatives and parental contemporaries. The idea was to introduce the young lady to gentlemen among whom she might one day find an appropriate spouse.

All this, however, changed after World War I. The parties swelled to enormous size, some to as much as a thousand or more, requiring rented ballrooms in town and marquees in the country, popular jazz orchestras, and oceans of champagne. The debutantes might be limited to the honoree's friends and acquaintances, but the men (often three times the number of the women to ensure a lively turnover on the dance floor) were selected from the lists of party givers. Gate-crashing was universal: I recall a checker protesting to one young man: "But I've already let in three Michael Graces!" Fathers came to pray that their daughters would not select a mate from among the young men present.

Yet for many a debutante, her party was the most important event of two years of her life, the deb and post-deb period. Few of them looked forward to careers other than marriage; many of them eschewed college or simply took a couple of courses in art history. I recall one deb, lovely and popular, who burst into uncontrollable sobs when a comedian, hired to entertain the guests during dinner, turned out to be a vulgar clown. But to the end of her unfortunately brief life she never regretted the effort that had gone into her party. She made the rich marriage she had hoped to make and was thoroughly happy in it. Those were different days.

The picture of two lovely sisters who came out together in a joint party during the Great Depression, Katherine and Joan Blake, is tinged for me with a certain sadness. I seem to see behind the blandness of their pose the faintest apprehension that theirs is a curious preparation for a future that may be many things, but will certainly be different. One made a great marriage by the standards of her world, but it failed. Reduced in means, she went to work and became a successful banker. The other did not marry until much older, but she was happy in her match and turned herself into a competent novelist.

Even in hard times, the older members of a debutante's family—grandparents or great-aunts—would open up old mansions long closed or maintained on a minor scale and staff and decorate them with their former magnificence. I recall such a party at the Breakers in Newport and being dazzled at the idea that my generation, into whose ears had been constantly dinned the idea that we were living at the end of an era, should find ourselves dancing and drinking in such marbled magnificence. Not even old-timer Henry White-house, who pointed to the empty grand staircase and told me that in the Gay Nineties every other step had been adorned by the presence of a footman, could dim for me the fineness of the scene.

It took a long time for historians and sociologists to recognize just how powerful was the effect of movies on our morals and folkways. Gore Vidal, in his novel *Hollywood,* describes an early film director, contemplating the vast power that he has to hand, as "knowing what God must have felt when he gazed upon chaos with nothing but himself on his mind." I used to tell Vidal that he was going too far in his evocation of a celluloid society, but when the American electorate in 1981 placed a movie star in the White House, I had to eat my words.

The star system made public heroes and heroines of our actors. Their "private lives," invented if necessary by experts in public relations, provided romance for a nation, and their beautiful faces and figures and even more beautiful clothes set new standards for looks and high living. How could the illustrators of fashion not have adored them? They were always cooperative; they lived to be photographed, and they knew just how to pose. Furthermore, their manners were easy and cordial, much more so than those of society folk, and no research was needed as to who and what they were. A dress worn by Joan Crawford was easier to sell than one by Mrs. William Rhinelander Stewart.

Joan Crawford might almost have been the symbol of the American woman of her era. She was Mildred Pierce, the humbly born girl with the will of granite to obtain all the good things of the world: status and riches and power, and love, too—oh, yes, love as well. And her noble, forcefully molded profile, always emphasized in her pictures, was an ample preview of her assured success. Success, however, was no guarantee of happiness. But that hardly mattered. She fascinated us in all her phases.

If Joan Crawford represented the American woman, Katharine Hepburn was the exemplar Yankee lady. She was one of the first to cross from the right side of the railroad tracks to the one where movies were made. Hollywood didn't know what to make of her for a while, but when she took her career into her own hands and demonstrated that she could be on the screen just what she was off it, a great star was made. Grinning at us from under a wide-brimmed straw hat on these pages, and balancing a picnic basket invitingly on her knee, she seems to be laughing at the artificiality of both movie and social spheres and suggesting that we go for a day's outing in the "real" world of nature.

But the peerless photograph, greatest of all in this volume, by Slim Aarons, is that of the four great male stars—Gable, Cooper, Stewart, and Van Heflin—easily but faultlessly clad in white tie and tails, drinking champagne at a party bar and laughing, genuinely laughing (even Cooper couldn't affect that grin) as they compose the very image of American he-men. You feel sure that they could strip off their finery and punch you in the nose the moment you got out of hand. And then go back to dazzle the ladies at the bar after their brief male recess.

What was the effect of all this affected naturalness beyond the movie screen? Look at Frick Byers: could such a picture have been taken of a social figure before the advent of the movie star? This handsome young horseman, arrayed in spotless white shirt and pants to set off the black of his lustrous hair and shiny boots, is posed with his back to a stall from which a gray mare reaches her head out to nuzzle his shoulder. And look, too, at Brian MacDonald, grinning so charmingly at us from the royal enclosure at Ascot, his gray top hat whimsically balanced on the tip of the tightly folded umbrella: both shots might be stills from forthcoming pictures. But they are beautiful.

Does anyone escape the eye-catching pose? Are we even sure, after so much fine photography, that we even want them to? Let us turn to the grande dames. Surely they will, if any. Lady Lindsay, American-born wife of the British ambassador, sits on the embassy porch in Washington in a straight-backed chair, her plump figure as stiff as a queen's, her knees and smartly slippered feet tight together. She holds a morsel sternly aloft until her small crouching dog shall obey some unheard command. Oh, yes, she is posing, but she is doing it with good humor and wit.

Mrs. Tommy Hitchcock is surely the "portrait of a lady," sitting on a porch in a green sweater and yachting cap and holding up a teacup in a strained pose that is obviously not of her choosing. She is rather afraid that she is making a fool of herself; she is doing it, one feels, at the persuasion of some younger relative or friend. And Alice Roosevelt Longworth gives us the stare she always gives: holding herself in reserve, waiting to see what idiotic question you will ask her. But she is still playing a role, the role she always plays—that of the Princess Alice.

What about the *petites dames*? What about the children? How do they fare in all of this? It is hard to tell, as they are so dressed up, so fetchingly posed. Major H. Stanley Cayzer's granddaughter perched on the front bumper of a splendid Rolls, Mrs. Arthur Pew's grandson cooperatively holding a basket as he assists her in her garden—what are they thinking? We don't know. They are doing what they are told. A few years later, when the boys arc fishing or sailing, we sense their enthusiasm, and even more so in the girls when they are riding, a sport that they take to young. The most revealing picture of all is of Stephanie Rodgers and Dyson Hepting, who can't be more than seven or eight, formally dressed and seated on two ballroom chairs against the wall, but with four empty chairs between them, their dangling feet not reaching the floor, exchanging a long, curious stare. Are they at a dancing class? Presumably. They seem too small for anything else. But what is entrancing is that they are not in the least interested in us or in the camera. They have eyes only for each other, the boy not yet quite sure why, the girl perhaps having a somewhat better idea.

The writers and artists, of course, are in a category all of their own. In these pictures one looks not for the setting or pose or for any particular beauty of feature but rather for such traces as we can make out of genius. One certainly senses it in the haggard eyes and grim lips of Erich Maria Remarque, and in the exquisite intelligence of Joseph Conrad's long, thin, trimly bearded physiognomy, and in the almost defiant pugnacity of Picasso's muscular figure and piercing eyes. One even sees it in the photograph confined to Stravinsky's wonderfully gesticulating hands. But the great picture of a writer—his return with hilarious vengeance to the world of fashion (literary fashion, at any rate)—

is that of "Papa" Hemingway at his supermacho best, being congratulated on bringing in a pair of monster marlins.

The real peak of fashion, however—socially, sartorially, financially, politically, even aesthetically—was the Kennedy-Bouvier wedding, the dawn of the era of Camelot. Toni Frissell took one of her greatest pictures of the bride and groom surrounded by the groom's ushers (no bridesmaids) at Hammersmith Farm in Newport. Some of the men are perched on a fence, some on the grass; the rest are gathered close around Jack and Jacqueline. The bride, beautiful as always, then even more so, in glorious organza and lace, is smilingly pointing to something we cannot see but which has made the whole group join her in a hearty laugh. The picture is replete with gaiety and cheer and courage and hope. It is heartbreaking.

But only because of how it ended. Camelot was something more than a sentimental label, it had a remarkable impact on a whole generation. I remember discussing the term with Walter Lippmann when it first appeared. I had thought he might be inclined to pooh-pooh it, but he insisted that the sort of charisma (and that was the word he used) that Jack and Jacqueline Kennedy exuded was a very rare and important political phenomenon, and something to be taken seriously by commentators. I suspected that he had failed to note it in Franklin Roosevelt and was not going to make that mistake again. It brings us back to my earlier observation by Napoleon. Fashion *is* power.

INDEX

PICTURE CREDITS

Page 3: M. Breckinridge. *Page 8:* Fotograms. *Pages 20–21:* Left, © Cynthia Matthews; right, Charles Langer. *Page 23:* Geoffrey Morris. *Pages 24–25:* Left, Alen MacWeeney; right, © Slim Aarons Foto. *Pages 26–27:* Underwood & Underwood. *Pages 28–29:* Left, International; right, Gray O'Reilly. *Page 30:* Top, November 15, 1934, *Town & Country;* bottom, Jerome Zerbe. *Page 31:* UPI/Bettmann. *Pages 32–33:* Donald Kennedy. *Pages 34–35:* Left, © John Lewis Stage; right, Tom Hollyman. *Pages 36–37:* Left, AP/Wide World Photos; right, Paul Thompson. *Pages 38–39:* January 1950, *Town & Country. Pages 40–41:* Left, Marvin Breckinridge; right, Pictorial News Co. *Pages 42–43:* © Slim Aarons Foto. *Pages 44–45:* Left, UPI/Bettmann; right, Robert W. Leavitt. *Pages 46–47:* Left, © Slim Aarons Foto; right, Geoffrey Morris. *Pages 48–49:* Left, October 1992, *Town & Country;* right, Andrew Eccles/Outline. *Pages 50–51:* Left, The Bettmann Archive; right, The Bettmann Archive. *Page 53:* Jerome Zerbe. *Pages 54–55:* Left, Brown Brothers; right, Brown Brothers. *Page 56:* October 20, 1906, *Town & Country. Page 57:* Top, January 1942, *Town & Country;* bottom, The Paul Thompson Collection. *Pages 58–59:* Brown Brothers. *Pages 60–61:* Left, Henry Morrison Flagler Museum Archives; right, Cameragrams. *Pages 62–63:* Top left, François Robert—Chicago; bottom, Dan Wynn; center, Jonathan Rawle; right, Robert Phillips. *Page 64:* Clockwise from top left, Freudy; Underwood & Underwood; Pamela Murray. *Page 65:* © Ronny Jaques. *Pages 66–67:* Left, © 1974 Fred J. Maroon; right, Robert Phillips. *Pages 68– 69:* Left, Paul Thompson; right, Skrebneski. *Pages 70–71:* Left, © Ronny Jaques; right, Jerome Zerbe, private collection. *Page 73:* © Ronny Jaques. *Page 74:* Clockwise from top left, February 1941, *Town & Country;* Jerome Zerbe, private collection; Jerome Zerbe, private collection; Jerome Zerbe, private collection; Jerome Zerbe, private collection. *Page 75:* © Paul Himmel, courtesy Howard Greenberg Gallery, New York City. *Pages 76 77:* Left, Louis Faurer; right, © 1996 Artists Rights Society (ARS), New York/ ADAGP/ Man Ray Trust, Paris. *Pages 78–79:* © Ronny Jaques. *Page 80:* Clockwise from top left, Max Peter Haas; European; Jerome Zerbe, private collection; Jerome Zerbe, private collection. *Page 81:* Clockwise from top left, Max Peter Haas; Jerome Zerbe, private collection; Jerome Zerbe, private collection; © Ronny Jaques. *Pages 82–83:* Left, Genevieve Naylor, courtesy Staley-Wise Gallery, New York; right, Photog. G.H. Huene © Horst. *Pages 84–85:* Left, © Ronny Jaques; right, © Slim Aarons Foto. *Page 86:* Left, © Ronny Jaques; right, © Ronny Jaques. *Page 87:* Clockwise from top, Luis Lemus; Luis Lemus; Eric Meacher. *Pages 88–89:* Left, Gleb Derujinsky; right, Serge Balkin. *Pages 90–91:* © Norman Parkinson/Hamilton Photographer/London. *Pages 92–93:* Left, © Ronny Jaques; right, Emerick Bronson. *Pages 94–95:* Left, Skrebneski; right, David Berns. *Pages 96–97:* Left, © Ronny Jaques; right, Magnum Photos, Inc. *Pages 98–99:* Left, © Ronny Jaques; right, Press Illustrating Service. *Page 101:* By Arnold Genthe. Garbo TM/© 1995 Harriet Brown and Company, Inc., all rights reserved, under license authorized by CMG Worldwide, Indianapolis, Indiana, USA. *Pages 102–103:* © Slim Aarons Foto. *Pages 104–105:* Left, Mario Testino; right, Philippe de Tellier. *Pages 106–107:* Left, F. Fonssagrives; right, Jean Moral. *Pages 108–109:* Left, Wendy Hilty; right, David Berns. *Pages 110–111:* Left, Desmond Russell; right, courtesy, the Estate of George Platt Lynes. *Pages 112–113:* Left, © Ronny Jaques; right, © Ronny Jaques. *Pages 114–115:* Left, © Ronny Jaques; right, F. Fonssagrives. *Page 116:* Left, Remie Lohse/Archive Photo; right, Jerome Zerbe. *Page 117:* Clockwise from top left, International; September 1935, *Town & Country;* © Ronny Jaques; International. *Pages 118–119:* Left, F. Fonssagrives; right, Geoffrey Morris. *Page 120:* Rotofotos. *Page 121:* Clockwise from top left, AP/Wide World Photos; Tom Kelley; © Slim Aarons Foto; Thelner Hoover. *Pages 122–123:* Left, © Slim Aarons Foto; right, Photograph by Matthew Rolston. *Pages 124–125:* Left, Frances McLaughlin-Gill; right, Bachrach. *Page 127:* Frances McLaughlin-Gill. *Pages 128–129:* © Slim Aarons Foto. *Pages 130–131:* Left, Toby Shure; right, Ronnie Kaufman. *Pages 132–133:* Left, David Berns; right, Anita de Braganca and Josephine Herrick. *Page 134:* Davis & Sanford. *Page 135:* Clockwise from top left, Aime duPont; Rochlitz; Harris & Ewing. *Pages 136–137:* Left, Luis Lemus; right, © 1995 Milton Greene Archive. *Pages 138–139:* Left, Jerome Zerbe; right, Jerome Zerbe. *Page 140:* Clockwise from top left, June 1962, *Town & Country;* January 1971, *Town & Country;* Moffett Studio; Jerome Zerbe. *Page 141:* Jerome Zerbe. *Pages 142–143:* Left, Luis Lemus; right, James Abbe, Jr. *Pages 144–145:* Left, February 1970, *Town & Country;* right, © Ronny Jaques. *Page 147:* Marceau. *Pages 148–149:* © Slim Aarons Foto. *Pages 150–151:* Left, Maria Von Matthiessen; right, Barbara Walz. *Pages 152–153:* © John Lewis Stage. *Page 154:* Clockwise from top left, International/Bettmann; July 15, 1933, *Town & Country;* Underwood & Underwood; Underwood & Underwood. *Page 155:* Clockwise from top left, Harris & Ewing; Curtis Bell; Herbert/Archive Photos; Burr McIntosh. *Pages 156–157:* Left, Tom Hollyman; right, Tom Hollyman. *Pages 158–159:* © 1975 Fred J. Maroon; right, Betsy K. Frampton. *Pages 160–161:* Left, Marc Riboud/Magnum Photos, Inc.; right, International Film Service. *Page 162:* Clockwise from top left, January 1971, *Town & Country;* John Rawlings; Stebbins, Chicago; Photo by Art Shay. *Page 163:* Tom Hollyman. *Pages 164–165:* Left, Martin Munkacsi, courtesy Joan Munkacsi and the Howard Greenberg Gallery,

New York; right, Underwood & Underwood. *Page 167:* February 3, 1912, *Town & Country. Pages 168–169:* © Dan Nerney 1983. *Pages 170–171:* Edwin Levick/Archive Photos. *Pages 172–173:* Left, Ivan Dmitri; right, AP/Wide World Photos. *Pages 174–175:* Anthony Edgeworth © 1995. *Page 176:* Clockwise from top left, photograph by Toni Frissell, courtesy Frissell Collection, the Library of Congress; Joseph Janney Steinmetz, courtesy Brett Arquette; Underwood & Underwood. *Page 177:* Eric Hedlind. *Pages 178–179:* Left, Art Seitz; right, Eugene Hutchinson. *Page 180:* Top, James H. Hare; bottom, Richard Carver Wood. *Page 181:* Top, January 1, 1927, *Town & Country;* bottom, Rittase. *Page 182:* Clockwise from top left, AP/Wide World Photos; Molly Cogwell; The Bettmann Archive. *Page 183:* © Cynthia Matthews. *Pages 184–185:* Left, Burton; right, Frederick Eberstadt. *Pages 186–187:* William Strode. *Page 188:* Top, February 1, 1934, *Town & Country;* bottom, courtesy of Canadian Pacific Limited. *Page 189:* Photograph by Toni Frissell, courtesy Frissell Collection, the Library of Congress. *Pages 190–191:* © Slim Aarons Foto. *Pages 192–193:* Left, Mrs. William Paley, photographed by Richard Avedon, 1957; right, © Howell Conant. *Page 195:* Baron de Meyer, collection of the J. Paul Getty Museum, Malibu, California. *Pages 196–197:* Left, Giuseppe Santoro; right, Curtis Bell. *Pages 198–199:* Left, Erica Lennard; right, Morgan Rank. *Pages 200–201:* Left, Baron de Meyer; right, Stephen Colhoun. *Pages 201–202:* Left, Stephen Colhoun; right, Stephen Colhoun. *Page 204:* Clockwise from top left, Dover Street Studio; Richard Brugiere; David Berns; AP/Wide World Photos. *Page 205:* Clockwise from top left, Anita de Braganca and Josephine Herrick; E. O. Hoppé; Ira Hill Collection, Archives Center, National Museum of American History; Bertram Park. *Pages 206–207:* Left, Gray Studio, Germantown; right, photograph by Toni Frissell, courtesy Frissell Collection, the Library of Congress. *Pages 208–209:* Photog. G.H. Huene © Horst. *Pages 210–211:* Left, UPI/Bettmann; right, E. O. Hoppé. *Pages 212–213:* Left, Ben Rose; right, Desmond Russell. *Pages 214–215:* Left, Baron de Meyer; right, Lee Miller Archives, London. *Pages 216–217:* Left, Genevieve Naylor, courtesy Staley-Wise Gallery, New York; right, Thomas Kublin. *Pages 218–219:* Left, © Slim Aarons Foto; right, photograph by Oberto Gili. *Pages 220–221:* Left, Herbert Gehr, *Life* Magazine, Copyright Time Inc.; right, Joe Covello. *Page 223:* Alfred Cheney Johnston. *Pages 224–225:* September 1, 1926, *Town & Country. Pages 226–227:* Left, © Milton Greene Archives; right, Ernst Schneider *(Berlin). Pages 228–229:* Left, March 30, 1907, *Town & Country;* right, Sam R. Quincey. *Page 230:* UPI/Bettmann. *Page 231:* Clockwise from top right; © 1996 Artists Rights Society (ARS), New York/ADAGP/Man Ray Trust, Paris; European Picture Service; E. O. Hoppé. *Page 232:* Clockwise from top right: Pacific & Atlantic; January 15, 1926, *Town & Country;* Kadel & Herbert. *Page 233:* UPI/Bettmann. *Pages 234–235:* Henry L. McNally. *Page 236:* Patrick O'Higgins. *Page 237:* Clockwise from top right, April 12, 1902, *Town & Country;* December 5, 1908, *Town & Country;* November 1, 1902, *Town & Country. Pages 238–239:* Left, © Milton Greene Archives; right, John C. Manning, Jr. *Page 240:* Clockwise from top left, AP/Wide World Photos; Central News Photo Service; Gloria Braggiotti Etting; June 1, 1931, *Town & Country. Page 241:* Clockwise from top left, April 1, 1930, *Town & Country;* Lifshey Anderson; April 1, 1932, *Town & Country;* Berenice Abbott/Commerce Graphics Ltd, Inc. *Pages 242–243:* Left, © 1996 Artists Rights Society (ARS), New York/ADAGP/Man Ray Trust, Paris; right, Kadel & Herbert. *Pages 244–245:* Left, Karger-Pix; right, June 14, 1902, *Town & Country. Pages 246–247:* Kadel & Herbert. *Pages 248–249:* Left, by Edward Steichen reprinted with permission of Joanna T. Steichen; right, November 1970, *Town & Country. Page 251:* Eva Barrett. *Pages 252–253:* David Berns. *Pages 254–255:* Left, Nickolas Muray; right, Underwood & Underwood. *Page 256:* Clockwise from top left, Underwood & Underwood; Harris & Ewing; Keystone. *Page 257:* Clockwise from top left, Jay Te Winburn; Parker Studio; Matzene. *Pages 258–259:* Left, Studio de France; right, David Berns. *Pages 260–261:* Marceau. *Pages 262–263:* Left, Denis Reggie; right, November 1957, *Town & Country. Pages 264–265:* Top left, Joseph Janney Steinmetz, courtesy Brett Arquette; top right, Underwood & Underwood; bottom, American Press Association. *Pages 266–267:* Left, Ira Hill Collection, Archives Center, National Museum of American History; right, Photo-Star. *Pages 268–269:* Photograph by Toni Frissell, courtesy Frissell Collection, the Library of Congress. *Pages 270–271:* Left, Standard News; right, Jay Te Winburn. *Page 273:* © Arnold Newman. All *Town & Country* pages photographed by Kevin Noble; assistant, Patty Wallace. Reproductions by Ken Pelka.